Electronic Resumes

& Online Networking

How to Use the Internet to Do a Better ⎿arch,
Including a Complete, Up-to-Date Resou⎿e Guide

By
Rebecca Smith

CAREER PRESS
Franklin Lakes, NJ

ELECTRONIC RESUMES AND ONLINE NETWORKING
Cover design by Hub Graphics
Printed in the U.S.A. by Book-mart Press

To order this title, please call toll-free 1-800-CAREER-1 (NJ and Canada: 201-848-0310) to order using VISA or MasterCard, or for further information on books from Career Press.

The Career Press, Inc., 3 Tice Road, PO Box 687, Franklin Lakes, NJ 07417

Library of Congress Cataloging-in-Publication Data

Smith, Rebecca, 1960-
    Electronic resumes & online networking : how to use the Internet to do a better job search, including a complete up-to-date resource guide / by Rebecca Smith.
        p.   cm.
    Includes index.
    ISBN 1-56414-377-5 (pbk.)
    1. Résumés (Employment)--Computer networks.   2. Job hunting--Technological innovations.   3. Job hunting--Computer networks.
    4. Internet (Computer network)   I. Title.
HF5383.S634   1998
025.06'65014--dc21   98-37045

Dedication

To Ernest L. Smith (1930-1997):
May this book inspire those who read it, just as you inspired me to write it.

Acknowledgments

Writing a book is never a one-person effort.

I want to thank all of those who let me share their personal anecdotes with my readers. This added a diverse and humanistic aspect to online technology. On the surface can appear cold and intimidating. But underneath, it is teeming with people just like you and I.

I want to thank Joyce Lain Kennedy who "discovered" me in a small corner of Cyberspace. Her encouragement and guidance was just what I needed to transfer my thoughts into words, of which this book is the result.

I would like to acknowledge the support and editorship of Trish McDermott and Helene Das at Desktop Effects. Their collaboration and reconstruction suggestions were invaluable to me. Other areas particularly helpful included their testing and editing of the tutorials in this book (a mammoth task in itself), verifying URLs to ensure they existed at the time of publication, and producing and staging the screen captures.

Thanks especially to the entire staff at Career Press: to Betsy Sheldon for adding her editorial magic; Ellen Scher who operated behind the scenes to make this book special; and John O'Sullivan, who made the final editing process an incredibly fun experience.

A very special thanks to David Fugate, my agent at Waterside Productions, for believing in me and in this project—which is my first.

And thanks to my husband Mike, who believed in me from the first day we met.

Contents

Foreword

If you're trying to move up and you don't acquire the know-how to track down the best jobs and craft resumes that can lasso them, you'll leave career opportunities on the table.

That's because the job-search process is getting a makeover—and the new look is dramatic! Think back in time. Until a few years ago, a number of career specialists convinced many job-seekers to throw away their resumes. They insisted that resumes weren't critical—or even particularly useful—in landing good jobs. They said that job-seekers should forget about resumes, that it was far more important to build relationships with people who had inside knowledge of potential job leads. The terms "networking" and "information interviewing" became buzzwords in job-search vernacular.

The Internet has put a giant-sized dent in that perspective. *Who* you know is important, yes, but sometimes crossing each bridge from person to person takes too long or just doesn't move you where you want to go. That's why the electronic resume is today's dynamic form of communication in a changing job market. That's why online job-searching is rapidly becoming online job-finding. That's why job seekers everywhere are firing up their computers and saying, *"Web, show me the jobs!"*

In the information age, resumes and job leads stand at the epicenter of the job market. Rebecca Smith zeros in on the facts clearly, being the first analyst to recognize an interrelationship between computer technology, resume development, and job location in both the unpublished and the published job market—a symbiotic convergence she describes as *resume networking*.

In the first book to combine this critical trio of elements into an integrated strategy, Becky explains that resume networking includes:

- *Targeting the online job market.* In Chapters 1 and 2, Becky explains how the job market for your type of work shapes your message and how the Net helps to join employers with an inventory of jobs and the people who want them.

- *Targeting your resume's content.* In Chapter 5, Becky brings home the important truths about marketing yourself—in your job field—to online recruiters.
- *Targeting your resume's distribution.* In Chapter 4, and Chapters 6 through 10, Becky demystifies ways to engage the attention of hiring managers by adroit selection of electronic destinations.

Throughout this original work, Becky Smith explains how you can use resume networking to move well beyond traditional face-to-face informational interviewing by mining the information-rich resources of the Net for job leads.

Afraid that you won't know what she's talking about? Don't be. Becky takes you by the hand and leads you comfortably through the wilds of the technology jungle. A trainer and teacher, Becky outdoes every other author in the detail and point-and-click directions offered in her mold-breaking guide.

Already, the author has become a favorite of Web reviewers across the world for the instructive resume tutorial on her award-winning eResumes & Resources Web site (www.eresumes.com). Based on overflowing positive feedback from appreciative tutorial-takers, Becky's guidance is awe-inspiring. According to a fan to whom Becky is a kind of employment angel:

> *"As an experienced 'paper' job-seeker who has few clues about the computer, I consider your page a religious experience. Thank you for being there. I think I will finally get responses to my e-mail resumes."*

I expect that you will also be offering praise to the heavens after you read the strategies and techniques Becky expounds in this book.

A bromide advising you how to buy computers is also useful for buying job search books: Buy for the future, not the past. Studies pop up every couple of weeks reporting that the vast majority of employers are going online to scout talent.

The individual who does not develop a coherent mastery of resume networking—using the computer to find plumb jobs on the Internet, then targeting your resume to the people who control those jobs—is at a severe disadvantage in new-century-style job search. With this book, you can get on the bus. The supersonic bus!

Joyce Lain Kennedy
Careers Columnist
Los Angeles Times Syndicate
San Diego, California
January, 1999

P.S. Even if you are the world's coolest computer authority, you need this book. Using a computer to market yourself requires a different kind of thought process than that used for proficiency in information technology.—JLK

Introduction

This book is not about resume writing. It's about how to take the content of an existing resume so that it is usable in an electronic form.

This book is not a discussion on how many people are actually getting jobs on the Web. Rather, it addresses the need of knowing how to use the tools available to you on the Internet to find job leads and then apply for those jobs.

This book shows you how to become a "remote insider" to gather information, and how to use that information to tailor and distribute a resume that gets noticed in a variety of electronic situations. The purpose of a resume to market your skills and abilities in a way that produces interviews has not changed. What has changed is the world in which we live with respect to technology. Technology is complex, but it does not have to be complicated. The electronic resume provides innovative ways of getting noticed in an increasingly online job market, where electronic file format is as important as style in presenting your qualifications, and the Internet can act as a multiplier on the effectiveness of your resume. This is the first book to combine job networking, resume development, and computer technology into one integrated strategy. This strategy is what I call "resume networking," and goes beyond traditional face-to-face networking and resume development.

Stedman Graham, author and keynote speaker who addressed University of California alumni during a UC Alumni Career Conference, says that "success is directly related to the options you have." Put the Internet and electronic resumes in context of your other job-search options; they are most effective when integrated with other self-marketing techniques in a coordinated job search campaign. When placed in the context of your other job-searching options.

In today's wired world, the Internet is valuable not just for finding jobs, but for finding out who is hiring, what skills are in demand, and how much those skills are worth. What's more, you can view other people's resumes right online, and attend chat sessions to find out more about your industry and how to compete. Will this diminish the need for traditional resume writing services, recruiters, and even Sunday paper delivery? No one really knows. But one thing is for certain: Careful planning, strategic resume posting online, and routine monitoring are some of the best guarantees in competing in this new kind of entrepreneurial job market.

Chapter 1

The Anytime Anywhere Online Job Market

Internet technology has undoubtedly had an impact on resume development and job networking and their effectiveness in uncovering hidden job opportunities. The Internet provides instant access to job market intelligence, such as who is hiring, what skills are in demand, and how much those skills are worth—24 hours a day. What's more, you can even view other people's resumes, attend discussion sessions, and browse corporate job postings directly. For the first time ever, individual job-seekers have access to the same information once only available to corporate insiders and recruiters.

In the days when the number of job-seekers exceeded the number of available jobs, recruiters always initiated the relationship. The job-seeker, anxious to keep options open, was expected to be ready and waiting for the phone to ring. However, all indicators point to the fact that the United States is now experiencing an employee's job market. This change in the balance of power has occurred in tandem with the evolution of the World Wide Web as a recruiting tool.

As all companies large and small expand their operational efficiency with computers, it will be necessary for job-seekers to expand their computer competency to online job-searching and resume-posting. The Internet also provides job-seekers with a way to contact more of the *right* employers in less time and, therefore, build a larger network of potential job leads.

A new kind of job market

Although newspapers and trade publications remain the medium of choice for job advertisements, more and more hiring managers and recruiters are going online to scout for job candidates. Why? Because it's cheaper, faster, the selection of candidates is much broader, and access is available 24 hours a day.

A good way to understand how the online job market works is to look at it in relationship to a typical job-search process. In the past, a typical job-search scenario went like this: You typed up your resume, sent it out in the mail to several employers from a list you made from the newspaper, and then waited a week or two. At that time, you may or may not have received a postcard in the mail notifying you that your resume was on file—whatever that meant. Before the Web, you could mail out dozens of paper resumes with no results.

Consider this scenario: A copy of the Sunday classified section reveals one job ad for Adobe Systems, Inc. Now visit Adobe's home page on the World Wide Web on that same Sunday, and you will find more than 150 jobs listed, the majority of which are located in your region. And those jobs can be listed on the Web at a fraction of what they would cost to print in your local newspaper.

Jobs are created on a daily basis, many times resulting from a decision at a corporate meeting. Traditionally, only an "insider" knew about these openings. The Internet now lets job-seekers become "remote insiders."

For the first time, individual job-seekers have access to the same kinds of information once only available to corporate insiders and recruiters. The Internet expands this process to include strategic uses of information on behalf of both the employer and job-seeker. The Web offers a vast amount of information that is unique to your industry and lets you target your job search.

Searching for jobs online gives informational interviewing a whole new meaning. It takes advantage of the informational value of the Internet without the anxiety often associated with scheduling and conducting such interviews. You will learn how to gather information and how to use that information to tailor and distribute a resume that gets noticed. The printed word, whether in e-mail messages or Web pages, is just as valuable as face-to-face interaction for uncovering job leads.

Used properly within the context of your other job-search options, the Internet may be the most cost-effective and efficient job-hunter's tool. Job-seekers are hopping online because they find their choices dramatically increased, and they have access to much more information.

The new online resume networking strategy

What else has changed? You can now make your resume work for you 24 hours a day. On the Internet, electronic resumes have become a form of ongoing communication between you and potential employers.

Traditional job-search books address job networking and resume development as separate processes independent of each other:

1. Resume development involves the resume-writing process so that the ultimate objective is to get interviews.
2. Job networking involves gathering information regarding job leads, where the ultimate objective is to gain access to the hidden job market.

On the Internet, these processes converge. This convergence requires a new way of thinking in order to take full advantage of the Internet as an effective job-search tool.

The Internet provides a new level of access to that hidden job market. Job networking online is different: *Whom* you know is not as important as where you go online to let people know about you and your skills.

Job networking online also provides the basis for two things:

1. It goes beyond traditional face-to-face *informational interviewing* by expanding on the information-giving resources of the Internet as potential sources of job leads.

2. It provides a basis for using electronic resumes to communicate between recruiters and job-seekers in many online situations.

The idea behind the new resume networking strategy is this: Just as businesses use information to develop their marketing plans to meet customer needs, job-seekers can use that information to tailor their resumes to meet employer need—and in less time. In today's constantly evolving job market, a job-seeker requires the same market intelligence that a small business owner requires to plan for and sustain a business for many years to come. In your case, it is to sustain a career. Meeting the needs of customers is the basis of all business. Meeting the needs of employers is the basis for getting hired. In other words, the job-search process is very much like the business-planning process: Identify a career focus, research the specifics of how the job market will support that career, and refine this information into measurable skills and accomplishments that will position you as the best person for the job. Your resume documents this process. The objective statement, whether you submit it on paper or keep it in your head, serves as your mission statement.

Faith Popcorn, the author of *Clicking: 17 Trends that Drive Your Business—and Your Life* (HarperBusiness), explains that a fad is short-lived and involves very few people. A trend, on the other hand, is big and broad, involving a lot of people, and can last 10 years or longer. Online job-searching is definitely not a fad, but a growing trend.

One thing is for certain—online job-searching won't go away anytime soon. Just as an entrepreneur looks to the future to determine today's marketing strategy, so must the person in search of a job in today's constantly changing job market. The new job market requires that the focus shift from finding a specific job to finding opportunities that support individual career goals. The Web is an ideal tool for this. The "jobpreneur's" objective is to present his or her qualifications in a way that reflects what he or she can do. In an online world, this takes on a whole new dimension.

The art of resume networking involves three principles that are introduced here. The chapters that follow will assist in your understanding of the Internet as an effective resume networking tool:

1. Know how employers are using it to attract and find candidates.

2. Recognize the technologies used to submit resumes online.

3. Identify ways to exploit the interactivity of the Internet for its job networking potential.

Online networking does not replace the value of face-to-face networking, and electronic resumes do not replace paper ones. However, they both give you a powerful edge in staying in touch with your industry in an increasingly wired world.

What does *online* mean?

What exactly does the term *online* mean? *Online* is any place that computer-users go via modems and telephone lines to meet with one another. Online can be a commercial service, such as America Online, that offers proprietary features such as chat rooms where many members connect to a central system to gather information and exchange ideas. Online can be a local or national Internet Service Provider (ISP) that offers subscribers local telephone access numbers. Online can be an electronic mail service, such as MCI Mail or AT&T Mail, that individuals use to send messages to online service users.

Two Internet components for job searching

The two most popular components of the Internet are the World Wide Web and electronic mail, also known as e-mail.

The World Wide Web

The terms "Internet" and the "World Wide Web" are often used interchangeably, although they are two entirely different things. The Web is a diverse collection of electronic documents stored on computers worldwide. Your computer can access these documents with an Internet connection and Web browsing software.

A Web browser is considered a *client* within the context of a client/server arrangement used on a network. Web documents are stored on a Web server that provides centralized storage services to the clients on that network. To better illustrate this, think of the following analogy: Let's say you open a pizza restaurant. The customers order a certain kind of pizza from a waiter. The waiter, who acts as a go-between, sends the order for pizza from the customer to the cook. The kitchen is where the cook reads the order, makes the requested pizza, and sends it to the waiter. The waiter then provides the pizza to the customer.

Now, let's tie this to the Web. In this example, the customer is the *user* of the pizza *services*. The waiter is the *client*, which in computer lingo is a software program (such as Netscape Navigator or Microsoft Internet Explorer) that searches for and uses services on the network. The cook in the kitchen is the *server* that provides centralized preparation and storage services to the client. In this case, the cook *server* gives the waiter *client* the completed pizza *services* on the restaurant *network*. These services in the Internet can include anything from news to shopping orders.

A Web browser knows how to go out onto the Internet in search of Web services. Web browsers enable you to browse the contents of the World Wide Web. Chapters 8, 9, and 10 will go into an extensive exploration of Web browsers.

The landscape of the online job market will increasingly become more Web-based as the Web matures and more people go online. The true advantage of finding jobs on the Web is that there is no software that needs to be loaded onto a PC. All that is needed by both employer and job-seeker to find each other is a Web browser and an Internet connection. Anyone can access the Web from any computer, at anytime, and from anywhere in the world.

E-mail and Internet service providers

The other popular component of the Internet is e-mail, which is a private message sent from one person to another person or persons via an online network. In simplest terms, e-mail is a message that is composed, addressed, and sent using a computer. More information about sending and receiving e-mail can be found in Chapter 6.

Most online service providers offer Internet access and some form of Internet e-mail. Internet access is available to anyone who has a computer and a modem. There are three main categories of Internet service providers that can provide you access to the Internet:

1. Commercial online services.
2. National Internet service providers.
3. Local Internet service providers.

Each kind of service offers varying degrees of content quality, Internet access, and support in learning the different interfaces and commands when configuring your PC's Internet applications (such as a Web browser, USENET newsgroup readers, e-mail program, etc.). When selecting a provider, consider your needs first. Some providers charge a flat fee or a separate fee depending on whether you use your account for personal or business uses.

Commercial online services, such as America Online, CompuServe, Prodigy, and Microsoft Network, make accessing the Internet easy. They offer parental controls, and a more structured, organized, and proprietary interface.

National Internet service providers, such as MCI Internet or AT&T WorldNet Service, serve large geographic regions. Local Internet service providers are found locally and provide the most direct access to the Internet. Depending upon the provider, they can offer the most Internet hours for the least money. Local providers are targeted to experienced users, but offer more of a personal touch.

There are a variety of sites on the Web that will help you find an online service provider that will fit your needs and your budget. ISPs.com (`http://www.isps.com`) lets you search national and local ISPs by price, name, and area code. The List (`http://www.thelist.com`) provides a list of providers in your area.

Another way to gain access to the Internet is to get online at your local library. Visit the Libweb (http://sunsite.berkeley.edu/Libweb/index.html) to find a library in your area. This resource maintains an exhaustive directory of more than 2,300 library home pages on the Web in more than 70 countries. Once you find a library in your area, contact it by e-mail or phone to inquire if it provides terminals with public access to the Internet, which in many cases is free, but with a time limit. If you don't have access to a computer connected to the Internet, consult your local phone directory for the name of your local libraries, and contact them directly.

Or go out and try an Internet cafe. Internet cafe shops, found in many major cities, offer Internet access in a coffeehouse environment. Yahoo! has a large list of Internet cafes included in its directory. Type in the keywords "Internet cafes" in the search field to go to these listings. Internet cafes, also known as "cyber cafes," provide Internet access usually charged on an hourly basis, with a food menu to boot.

Finding your online starting points

The specific Web resource that you decide to send your resume to will determine how you prepare your resume before submitting it electronically. You might start out with the online version of the employment classifieds from your local newspaper. You can find out who is hiring by doing a keyword search through the classified's database. The listings will usually have a link to the employer's Web site. If not, simply type the employer's name into a search engine to find it. Once you arrive at the Web site, you'll find not only more job listings, but instructions on how to prepare and submit your resume —electronically.

Let's take a look at the following four popular categories of online employment resources:

1. Search engines (including subject directories and lookup directories).
2. Media sites (trade magazines and classified advertisers).
3. Job boards (recruitment firms; third party matching services; career hubs).
4. Virtual job fairs.

These starting points are listed in the order of how much information you will find there: from general information about jobs worldwide, to specific details about employers with actual jobs you can apply for. By organizing information on the Web in this manner, you can better target employers with jobs for specific industries and geographic locations, identify the skills needed to do those jobs, and tailor your resume before applying for those jobs online. These four categories are starting to combine with other resources on the Web, forming "portals." Portals combine all of the popular elements of the Web—search engines, career sites, news headlines, free e-mail, and more. Many of the popular search engines now serve as gateways to popular job boards. Following, each category is described in terms of how to recognize it on the World Wide Web.

1. Search engines

Search engines are the best online starting points to find relevant Web sites. You can type in the keywords relevant to your industry such as "culinary industry" or "culinary jobs."

Browsing and searching are the most common activities on the Web. According to Georgia Tech Research Corporation's Sixth GVU (Graphic, Visualization, and Usability Study) Web User Survey (http://www.cc.gatech.edu/gvu/user_surveys) for October 1996, 77 percent of the 15,000 respondents surveyed said that browsing was their primary activity on the Web. When asked what strategies they used when browsing, 78 percent said they use search engines to find information on the Web.

Many of these sites have expanded by building affiliations with other content providers. Important to job-seekers is the fact that these search engines are also integrating job listings to their sites.

- **Alta Vista** (http://www.altavista.com), for example, not only lets you search Web pages and postings to USENET newsgroups by keywords, it also has a Career Zone at http://www.careeraltavista.com/ where you can search for and post resumes and jobs.
- **Excite** (http://www.excite.com) provides access to company profiles. This site offers access to The Monster Board (http://www.monsterboard.com) to find a job and build a resume.
- **HotBot** (http://www.hotbot.com) acts as a gateway to the Web site CareerBuilder Network (http://www.careerbuilder.com).
- **Infoseek** has a special career section that takes you to Careerpath.com (http://www.careerpath.com) to find and post jobs.
- **Lycos** has teamed up with **Tripod** to serve as a gateway to the Careers Web Guide with links to Career Guides for Winners, and CareerMosaic to search jobs and post resumes.
- **WebCrawler** (http://www.webcrawler.com) offers a Careers category where you can browse or search from career-related categories. It also provides a gateway for you to post resumes and search jobs at the Classifieds2000 Web site (http://www.classified2000.com).
- **Yahoo!** (http://www.yahoo.com) features employment classifieds, with free job postings and searches. Yahoo! has also integrated into its directory the "Submit Ads for Employment Wanted." You can register by going to http://classifieds.yahoo.com/employment.html and by selecting the "Submit Ad" link at the top of the page. Once you have registered, you can submit an Employment Wanted ad by filling out the online form.

2. Media sites

Media sites are online equivalents of newspapers and trade magazines. They allow users to purchase products, read product reviews, play games, and download software. They also provide a forum to interact with like-minded people, depending on the focus of the magazine. These resources are especially valuable to job-seekers in that they focus job leads by geographic location and industry.

Electronic Newsstand (http://www.enews.com) bills itself as the ultimate magazine source, allowing you to find your favorite magazine online. Mediafinder (http://www.mediafinder.com/index.cfm) is a metaresource for finding links to magazines, newsletters, journals, and newspapers. Many online versions of magazines offer discussion forums, chat rooms, and career resources targeted to their readership.

Also, many newspapers have established an online presence that supplements their print version. These are especially beneficial for searching classified advertising, where you are provided additional resources to research the companies that are listing their job postings.

One way to take advantage of media sites is to scour print and online classifieds for leads to companies that have home pages on the Internet. Check out Career-Path.com, which lists more than 20 major newspapers with online classified employment advertising; Classifieds2000 (http://www.classifieds2000.com); The Wall Street Journal (http://www.wsj.com); or a regional trade magazine such as *Computer Bits* (http://www.computerbits.com/gateway/jobs.htm), serving the Oregon high-tech industry.

3. Job boards

Job boards are hosted by recruiters, employment agencies, and marketing or advertising firms specializing in the job-search industry. They are also referred to as matching services and career hubs. These kinds of resources are valuable to job-seekers for narrowing down job leads by company.

Job boards typically work like this: Employers post job ads and search through resumes. Job-seekers search the job ads and post their resumes. Depending on the resources used, either of these activities may be free—or there may be a service fee.

Good online starting points are c|net's search.com (http://www.search.com). Select the "Employment" category, where you can search more than 30 different job boards one at a time, but all in one place. Also Weddle's Web Guide (http://www.nbew.com/weddle.html) is a very good resource. It provides a comprehensive listing of the major job boards where you can post your resume. It also provides information on how many jobs are posted, how many resumes are posted, and if the resource charges a fee or is free. Refer to Appendix A for a comprehensive listing of additional job boards.

4. Virtual job fairs

Virtual job fairs are an extension of corporate Web sites. However, they serve a different purpose because they have a face-to-face component to them. With virtual job fairs, you can research participating companies online before attending the job fair in person. They provide a calendar of upcoming fairs for a particular geographic area and a list of what companies are participating. By following the links provided to the corporate Web sites, you will find hundreds of job ads. Browse the jobs listed, determine if you have the qualifications to apply for each, and tailor your resume accordingly. If you cannot attend the job fair in person, you can post your resume to the fair's online database. If you can attend, you will be prepared ahead of time to meet face-to-face with recruiters. This targeted information gives you a powerful edge when you meet with the hiring managers personally. Not only will you have a more complete knowledge of what their hiring needs are, you will also have a tailored resume ready if you are called in for an onsite interview.

Virtual job fairs are excellent resources for finding out who is hiring ahead of time, and what their hiring needs are. They are a good opportunity to network with many companies at once. They allow you to find out about participating companies, contact the recruiters, and ask questions about the firm. If you don't have the connections, this is a chance to make them. Job fairs benefit hiring managers because they can obtain a large amount of candidate resumes in the shortest amount of time. Job fairs attract job-seekers because they serve as a one-stop source of potential employers who have actual hiring needs. Instead of standing in line, you can get a feel for the job fair ahead of time.

To find out more about who is hiring and for what positions, consider the following example: Westech's Virtual Job Fair (http://www.careerexpo.com) provides a calendar of upcoming fairs for any area. Westech's site provides an Exhibitor's list of participating companies with links to their home pages. Visit the home pages of prospective employers; you will find more links to employment listings for that company. Browse the job listings that interest you, determine if you have the qualifications to apply, and tailor your resume accordingly.

Remember, the hiring process is just as time-consuming as the job-search process. The more informed and better prepared you are as a job-seeker, the easier you make it for hiring managers to screen your application. You benefit because your preparation conveys your resourcefulness and level of interest in meeting their hiring needs. Refer to Appendix A for a list of virtual job or career fairs. These all serve as excellent starting points.

Chapter 2

Targeting Your Online Job Search

With more than 60,000 career sites listing more than one million jobs, you can be assured that there are more choices in the job marketplace than ever before. This also means you will have to pay more attention to what each online resource has to offer. With every opportunity comes the daunting task of separating *useful* information from irrelevant data and deciding how to use that information to meet your career objectives.

One way to obtain valuable information is to organize your search around specialized rather than general employment topics. You can do this by starting with the major Web search engines, but targeting specialized job boards, researching specific industry-related online news publications, and then drilling down to employer Web sites with specific job listings. By keeping your search organized, you can prioritize what online resources you want to search, and then filter out the useless data.

Assess your skills to do the job

Before you start any serious job search, you first need to list the skills that you have, and whether they match the needs of your target job. You can do this by using the Internet to keep in touch with your trade.

You can use this information to update your resume. It helps you target your resume with the skills you need by researching the job descriptions.

You can also use this specialized information to determine whether you make a good fit for the job in the first place. Just by browsing job listings, you can get a feel for what skills are required for a specific job. You can then tailor your resume to show how your skills match an employer's needs. Consider what Richard Jowsey, a senior software engineer, has to say of his online job searching experience:

"It's hard to go out 'selling' oneself after many years of being happily employed in a good firm. When I read through (online) job vacancies, I realized there's so much I don't know yet, which can be fairly bloody discouraging! Getting my objectives and 'core competencies' figured out has been a big help. At least I can now quickly eliminate 99 percent of the positions being offered, and not try stretching myself to fit in where I'm probably going to be unhappy anyway."

Take advantage of specialized job boards

Job boards are becoming more and more popular because they allow businesses to recruit directly without the added cost of headhunter fees. Some may argue that posting jobs on the Internet restricts the employer/recruiter to people who have a computer-related background. But job services are expanding into other industries, including nursing, law, accounting, finance, teaching, aviation, and even funerary services.

Refer to Appendix A for a list of industry-specific job boards currently on the Web. You will see that both technical and nontechnical, small and big businesses are going online everyday.

Specialized job boards can be either employment sites, or of special interest, such as a trade magazine online, with job listings as one of many other features. These sites take the form of online versions of magazines that also provide job listings targeted for their readership. Job-seekers should try and target these specialized job boards before visiting the larger metajob boards such as The Monster Board (http://www.monster.com) or America's Job Bank (http://www.ajb.dni.us)—their hundreds of job listings can become daunting to wade through.

When searching for information on your particular industry, start with two or three different search engines to see which ones return the most relevant results. One good way is to take advantage of metasearch engines such as Savvy Search (http://www.savvysearch.com) where you can use several search engines at once. Savvy Search is designed to send your query to multiple Internet search engines and return the complete set of results. To get an idea of what is out there in cyberspace, refer to Appendix A for a list of job boards currently on the Web. You will see that many businesses, regardless of industry or size, are jumping on the Web.

Obtain more information from corporate Web sites

Another good way to target your job search is to send e-resumes to corporate Web sites directly, if you know ahead of time what companies you would like to work for. Even big job boards like The Monster Board don't list all jobs. Instead, they may list company profiles with hyperlinks to corporate Web sites where the jobs are really listed.

Employers are beginning to see the benefits of Internet recruitment. According to the first Internet Recruitment Survey (http://www.ak.com/jobsurvy.htm) released by Austin Knight, an international recruitment and employee communications firm, 93 percent of the companies polled use the Internet as a recruitment tool. More companies will rely on their own Web site nowadays to post jobs to attract job applicants. The hundreds of job services that are online now may not be alive for long.

The job-seeker benefits from corporate Web sites, as well. He or she can obtain information about a particular job offer and learn more details about the company. Many employers now include a tag line in the newspaper employment classifieds to visit their Web site, where they will have additional jobs to offer and information about the company.

You may be able to access the company's annual report online. The annual report contains the history of the past year, corporate vision for the future, and other information. Take a look at IBM's annual report (http://www.ibm.com). You can even download and print the files to read later.

You can also find information on corporate history, benefits, and the workplace environment. You can prepare for that interview by researching press releases, product and service reviews, client testimonials, and other corporate publications.

At many of the corporate Web sites, you can learn about a firm's products, culture, and organizational changes. You can get a feel for a company's mind-set by what it tells the public. One company might tell its corporate history, while another might talk about teamwork. Texas Instruments (http://www.ti.com) offers "Fit Check," which lets you evaluate your personal and professional "fit" with the company's work environment and corporate culture. You're asked to read 32 statements and rate each one on a scale ranging from "Strongly Agree" to "Strongly Disagree." When you're done, you click on the **See the Results** button to receive a response.

Many governmental Web sites provide useful job information. For example, take a look at the Web Site from the U.S. Army Corps of Engineers in Baltimore (http://www.nab.usace.army.mil/index.html). Before browsing the list of current job vacancies, you can follow links to current projects and services, such as hazardous waste cleanup, civil engineering, and flood plain management.

A great service that corporate Web sites provide is the ability for candidates to talk to current employees. For example, the employee profile function on the Cargill Website (http://www.cargill.com/hr/recruit/Turkey.html) lets you meet specialists in the processing, marketing, and sale of turkeys. Not only do you find employee profiles and duties, you also get a glimpse of the natural career progression in this company—from initial training to supervisory opportunities.

Cisco (http://www.cisco.com), upon receiving your resume, will match you with a Cisco employee so you can get the inside scoop on what it is like to work there through the "Friends @ Cisco" online program. Cisco also lets you target what jobs are available, the organizational structure, and departments and functions. It will also find a particular department or division you might want to work in. You can then submit your resume directly to the department that you are interested in.

When you browse Cisco's employment page, you can elect to search for jobs by division or geographic location. This gives you an indication of how the company is organized, and what kinds of skills are needed to perform successfully in those departments. When you click on the **Show Jobs** button, you can browse all of the job listings, which also provides you with the e-mail addresses of contacts within that specific division.

To find companies that have home pages with job listings, use search engines and follow the links. Scour print and online classifieds for leads to companies that have home pages online. Refer to Appendix B for good online starting points.

Keep up with your profession in discussion forums and virtual communities

"Hanging out" at a forum with industry professionals is a great way to keep tabs on the latest business trends—and potential job leads. The growing number of both technical and nontechnical forums makes the Internet an ideal tool for building contacts, with thousands of opportunities to access industry experts on a variety of topics.

Forums are popular because they are devoted to specific subjects. Participating in online newsgroups, mailing lists, and Web-based forums can add a non-threatening dimension to "cold-calling." One of the biggest obstacles traditional to employment networking is the discomfort of making networking connections and socializing at networking events. Saying "I'm not looking for a job, just interested in knowing more about your company" doesn't sound very sincere these days. In contrast to face-to-face networking, online networking allows otherwise hesitant individuals the opportunity to learn about their intended market.

Newsgroups

Newsgroups are forums for discussion in which people exchange information by posting articles. Newsgroups are like giant bulletin boards—people post and reply to messages. Most newsgroup software can easily sort the messages by topic. These topics are called "threads."

There are more than 20,000 newsgroups, and this number keeps increasing. Your Internet Service Provider (ISP) has a news server that delivers news posts to you. The problem is, there is no one central place to store all of the world's posts. Because your ISP doesn't have unlimited storage space, it deletes posts once they reach a certain age. This can range anywhere from a few days to a few weeks old. Once they are deleted, they are gone forever. Bypass these limitations by accessing newsgroups from DejaNews (`http://www.dejanews.com`). It's the only Web site where you can read, search, participate in, and subscribe to more than 50,000 discussion forums, including Usenet newsgroups.

Within the Usenet, there are both official and unofficial groups. This process serves as a filtering mechanisms to weed out offensive and/or illegal posts, although not all unofficial newsgroups fall into these categories. Your ISP is almost certain to carry these official newsgroup posts. Unofficial newsgroups are easier to create, but your news server is not under obligation to carry them.

Newsgroups have names that look like a series of word (or abbreviations) separated by periods. For example:

```
nyc.jobs.contract
nyc.jobs.offered
nyc.jobs.wanted
```

These names go from general to specific (*contract, offered,* and *wanted* are the categories of jobs found in these newsgroups for New York City). Usenet regulates the way official newsgroups are named when created. Unofficial newsgroups are not regulated, but always begin with "alt" so they look like:

```
alt.medical.sales.jobs
alt.computer.consultants.ads
alt.journalism.criticism
```

When you set up your newsreader, (information on how to do this is provided by your ISP when you open your account), your newsreader should be able to search for the keywords you supply. For example, searching for "writing jobs" yielded:

```
alt.jobs
ca.jobs
chi.jobs
kc.jobs
seattle.jobs.offered
atl.jobs
dfw.jobs
```

You can usually access your newsreader from a current version of your favorite Web browser.

Mailing lists

Mailing lists, also called LISTSERVs, are a widely used Internet technology. Mailing lists are much like newsgroups, except that messages are mailed directly to your e-mail account. Where anyone with a newsreader can look at posts on a newsgroup, mailing lists are more exclusive and structured. Once you discover a mailing list you would like to be part of, you must request to be added to the list via e-mail. After you're added, you can send an e-mail to the list's central address, which will forward that message to everyone else on the list. Likewise, you will automatically receive e-mail that other members of the list send to the central address. All you need is an e-mail program and Internet access.

Jacqui Cook Greene, an internship coordinator for University of North Carolina-Chapel Hill, shares her favorite story about a student participating in a mailing list on rebuilding old cars. One of his e-mail acquaintances finally noticed the .edu of his e-mail address and asked if he was a student. It turned out that the student was communicating with an IBM vice president who offered him a summer internship in finance!

Mailing lists are more private and more reliable than newsgroups. On the other hand, they can take up a lot of room in your e-mail inbox.

A wonderful resource for finding mailing lists is the Publicly Accessible Mailing Lists page at http://www.neosoft.com/internet/paml/index.html. Another popular resource is the LISZT (http://www.liszt.com), a mailing list directory.

Currently, discussion forums on the World Wide Web can take the form of hierarchical, threaded-message discussion bases or real-time chat services on the Internet Relay Chat (IRC) network. Such forums are variations of nonWeb-based forums such as mailing lists and newsgroups. They are accessed directly from the World Wide Web without subscription requirements (mailing lists), or newsreader requirements (newsgroups). With the exception of real-time discussion forums on the IRC, the only requirement to participate in a Web-based forum is a browser and access to the Internet.

Web-based forums use software that republishes existing discussion databases into a hierarchical format. A participant can choose to read the different messages posted to the forum, initiate a new post, or respond to an existing post. Another advantage of these web-based forums is that you can visit them at anytime, and many provide an archival feature where you can search for previous discussions that took place. Real-time chat does not offer an archive of previous discussions.

Virtual communities

Virtual communities are different from forums because they include discussion forums targeted at specific groups of people. Members keep profiles in these communities, and many allow users to become forum leaders. Some of these popular online virtual communities include: Tripod (http://www.tripod.com), About Work (http://www.aboutwork.com), and ThirdAge Media (http://www.thirdage.com).

Strategic uses of metajob boards

If your targeted search doesn't reveal anything useful, then try the metajob boards that provide job listings and resume services for broader audiences. These metajob boards have evolved from job listings and resume databases for multiple specialty areas. They're large and more general than specialty job boards or corporate Web sites.

They, however, have their advantages. Job-seekers can conduct their own searches at popular job boards such as The Monster Board, and then go directly to a corporate Web site and apply there, completely bypassing The Monster Board's online registration form altogether. Look at these big job boards as mini-versions of search engines to discover links to potential employers or job opportunities that you might not have found otherwise.

The one-hour job search

Rather than wandering around in Cyberspace bookmarking what looks interesting, activate your search with a specific goal in mind. *Focus.* With the large volume of information available on the Internet, you are bound to get lost if you do not stay focused on the job at hand.

To give you an idea of what's out there for your particular profession or level of employment, the following three online job-search scenarios prioritize resources based on the kinds of relevant information found there that would support the representative career objectives.

Anya, the college graduate

This scenario involves Anya, a soon-to-graduate college student. With a degree in Business Administration, Anya is interested in electronic commerce. Her best bet is to search trade magazines to get a feel for the current trends in electronic commerce, study the postings at corresponding discussion forums, then search the job boards, job fairs, and corporate Web sites. These will give her leads on employers that hire entry level. Her research will arm her with "buzz words" needed to search the databases. The corporate Web sites will provide research content to help her prepare for interviews.

Her online research results in these "buzz words": electronic commerce; online shopping; intelligent software; e-commerce; retailing; permission marketing; mass customization; interface design. Anya collected a list of the following resources to help her begin an in-depth online job search:

Trade magazines and classifieds

CommerceNet

`http://www.commerce.net`

Provides research on emerging e-commerce business and technology trends and developments, offering networking opportunities with the key players in the market.

The Electronic Commerce Guide

`http://e-comm.internet.com`

Sponsored by IBM software e-business, provides information on organizations, government agencies, and user groups that offer electronic commerce services and products.

Hewlett Packard's E Business Magazine

`http://www.hp.com/Ebusiness/main1.html`

A good example of a corporate online publication that provides an "insider" look at HP's corporate perspective on the e-commerce industry.

The Wall Street Journal

`http://www.wsj.com`
`http://careers.wsj.com`

Find employers who are actively recruiting college graduates.

Discussion forums

eCommerce @lert

`http://www.cobb.com/eca`

A newsletter, Web site, and mailing list all rolled into one URL. Interact with people in this industry by visiting the message boards.

The Career Networking Group

`http://www.careerevents.com/fairs.html`

Provides links and information about newspaper-sponsored job fairs.

Job boards that target college graduates

Recruiting-links.com
`http://www.recruiting-links.com`
Search by location (national or worldwide), industry, and job function.

The Job Resource
`http://solimar1.stanford.edu`
Started by students from Stanford University in 1996, this is a service "run by students for students." It features companies recruiting college graduates.

JobTrak
`http://www.jobtrak.com`
A decade-old resource that targets the placement of college graduates in coordination with college Career Services Centers across the nation.

JobDirect
`http://www.jobdirect.com`
An Internet job service offering entry-level positions. Candidates are automatically alerted by e-mail when a position is posted that meets specifications they've entered. After following a link to get more information about a job, students can click on a response button to submit their resumes.

MBA Employment Connection Association
`http://www.mbanetwork.com`
Lists links to more than 190 recruiters that specialize in recruiting MBAs.

CareerPark
`http://www.careerpark.com/jobs/acctlist.html`
Accounting, investment, management, marketing, and sales jobs.

Recruiter's Online Network
`http://www.recruitersonline.com`
Recruiter listings for more than 70 specialty categories.

Alumni Network
`http://www.alumni-network.com`
Job openings for experienced and new grads. Network with other grads.

Virtual job fairs

Westech Virtual Job Fair
`http://www.careerexpo.com`
A California-based corporation specializes in high-tech career events and publications nationally since 1982.

The JobWeb Career Fairs Clearinghouse
`http://www.jobweb.org/cfairsr.htm`
Produces career fairs sponsored by member colleges of the National Association of Colleges and Employers.

The Lendman Group
http://www.lendman.com
Produces national Career Fairs since 1964.

The Monster Board Career Fair Information
http://www.monster.com/careerfair.html
Provides a calendar of career fair information.

Corporate Web Sites

Hewlett Packard
http://www.jobs.hp.com
A major computer company. A good example to explore different kinds of job opportunities with a company that has offices all over the world.

KPMG
http://www.kpmgcareers.com
Accounting firm. Go to college links to find information on interviewing with the company with jobs for electronic commerce consultants.

Andersen Consulting
http://www.ac.com/index.html
Consulting firm with jobs for business process managers.

Ernst & Young
http://www.ey.com
Accounting firm. Visit the *Idea Factory* for an example of a corporate Web site that invites visitors to join in on threaded discussion groups.

The Gap
http://www.gap.com
Retailer of clothing. A good site to study an example of a successful online retail sales process.

Greg the construction worker

Greg is trying to find a construction job in California. He's looking for residential or commercial building construction work on a permanent or contract basis, specializing in HVAC (heating, ventilating, and air-conditioning).

Greg is accessing a computer connected to the Internet at his local library because he does not own a computer of his own. He's not quite sure if he'll find any construction jobs—he's heard that the Internet is ideally suited for those who are seeking more technical professions, such as computers or engineering. Here are the resources he uses.

Subject directories

Greg starts his search by browsing through search engines just to see what's out there. He hopes to find information regarding job leads and/or potential clients.

Greg uses the same search terms for several different search engines. This gives him a feel for which search engine or directory will produce the kind of results he is looking for. He checks out the following search engines:

Savvy Search
http://www.savvysearch.com
Simultaneous search by keywords and subject of more than 20 search engines in 20 different languages.

Alta Vista
http://www.altavista.com
Search by keywords.

Yahoo!
http://www.yahoo.com
Search by subject.

Reader's Digest LookSmart
http://www.looksmart.com
Search by subject and keywords.

The keywords that Greg uses in his searches include: construction jobs; California homebuilders; HVAC; building; and construction.

On Yahoo!, Greg discovers "Business and Economy: Magazines: Trade Magazines." This Yahoo! category provides links to hundreds of industry-specific magazines found on the Web. In addition to Web resources, trade magazines are great for zeroing in on industry-related news.

Trade magazines

Greg refines his search by drilling down to the construction category to view a list of building-related trade magazines. He looks for references to current projects; job listings; contract positions; trade associations; discussion forums; and salary surveys at each site. He also scans the advertisers and subsequent links to Web sites for additional potential job leads. After browsing the list of results from the results obtained from his Yahoo! search, Greg links to some specific magazines that might have what he's looking for. By researching these trade magazines and "e-zines" (online versions of magazines), he is also able to zero in on industry-related key buzzwords. These buzzwords help him refine searches even more as he browses through more search engines, subject directories, and job boards.

The Electronic Newsstand
http://www.enews.com/monster
Links to more than 2,000 magazines.

BuilderOnline
http://www.builderonline.com
Residential construction industry.

Builder and Developer Magazine
http://www.bdmag.com
California residential building industry.

Engineering News-Record
http://www.enr.com
A construction weekly. Browse the job listings, which are updated frequently.

Buildings Online
http://www.buildingsmag.com
Researches trends and products in the commercial and institutional building industry. Find out about new building products and applications, trade shows, and other current events.

Job boards

Search.com
http://www.search.com
Greg can search more than 30 job boards one at a time, but all in one place. He selects the most job categories and keywords that might relate to his industry and geographic region.

JobSmart
http://www.jobsmart.org
Search job ads and job fairs for Northern California.

Net-Temps
http://www.net-temps.com/states/ca/index.html
Find employment recruiters in California.

Michael L. Ketner & Associates, Inc.
http://www.ketner.com
A search firm that specializes in the construction industry.

Greg searches for specific job ads listed by employers in the construction and building trades, possibly located in California. He also selects the most job categories and keywords that might relate to his industry to produce the greatest results. Then he narrows his search down from there.

Local newspaper classifieds

CareerPath.com (http://www.careerpath.com) lets Greg search newspapers in California to research current classified ads. By clicking on the jobs search link to search the help-wanted database by newspaper, job category, and keywords, Greg can find job leads instantly. He searches for construction jobs in Northern or Southern California in a recent Sunday edition of the paper, using the search feature provided at most online newspaper sites to link directly to the employment classifieds section.

San Jose Mercury News
`http://spyglass.sjmercury.com/class`
Employment information for Northern California.

Los Angeles Times
`http://www.latimes.com/HOME/CLASS/EMPLOY`
Employment information for Southern California.

Northern California Newspaper Classified Ads
`http://www.jobsmart.org/adjobs/newspap.htm`
Find employment information for specific counties in Northern California.

Corporate Web sites

Now that Greg is getting the hang of his online searching skills, he decides to research some of the hiring companies mentioned in the classified ads. Going back to Yahoo! to find a directory of company listings, he decides on CompaniesOnline (`http://www.companiesonline.com`), which provides links to thousands of public and private corporate Web sites. He uses this resource to find more detailed information about a preferred employer. For example, Greg searches for corporate Web sites such as Standard Pacific. He then finds out if they have a Web site, notes the URL, and visits the Web site to look for current employment and contract opportunities in California as well as specific job application details. Here are some others he finds:

Hoovers Corporate Web site
`http://www.hoovers.com`
Links to more than 4,000 corporate Web sites.

CompaniesOnline
`http://www.companiesonline.com`
Search thousands of companies online by industry.

The TRANE Company
`http://www.trane.com/index.html`
Ventilating and air-conditioning industry.

Standard Pacific, Inc.
`http://www.baynet.com/pacific/index.html`
National homebuilder with development projects in California communities.

Theresa, the management consultant

Theresa works in the international insurance industry as a management consultant, speaks English, Chinese, and Cantonese fluently, and wants to relocate from Asia to the United States, but is not sure where or how to start looking.

Her strategy is to focus on finding out current business and career trends for different industries in the United States, and what companies are doing business in both Asia and the U.S. for a particular industry within the management consulting discipline. Theresa starts with the different job boards to research actual job postings and potential employers.

Job boards and recruitment firms

NationJob Network
http://www.nationjob.com/management
Executive and management job listings updated weekly.

Online Career Center
http://www.occ.com/occ/Companies/A.html
Job listings by company name.

Recruiters Online Network
http://www.ipa.com
A recruitment firm that specializes in the management consulting industry.

Kane & Associates
http://www.jobmenu.com
This management recruiting firm provides a listing of positions in a variety of disciplines. A good resource to get a sense of job titles and skills in the U.S., and how to translate foreign skills and accomplishments accordingly.

Management Recruiters International
http://www.mrinet.com
A large international search and recruitment firm with more than 650 offices, specializing in placing "the best" executive, managerial, professional, and technical talent for their clients.

Theresa searches for job ads listed by employers that either specialize in management consulting or hire internal management consultants. Her overall strategy is to take advantage of the larger international/national recruitment firms and job board Web sites.

Newspaper classifieds

Theresa searches the employment classified sections for regional employers. She starts by focusing on the larger national papers, and then narrows her search down to the regional papers for her area of interest.

USA Today
http://www.usatoday.com
National headline news at a glance.

The Wall Street Journal
http://www.wsj.com
National business and finance news. Requires a subscription, but offers headline news and special features for nonsubscribers.

The Washington Post
http://www.washingtonpost.com
Regional East Coast news with a focus on the Nation's Capitol. Search the Job ads (http://www.junglee.com/twp/cat_loc.html).

San Jose Mercury News
http://www.mercurycenter.com
Regional West Coast news with a high-technology slant.

Trade magazines and e-zines

Theresa searches for business and employment trends in America. She also finds out about how global business in Asia and America overlap in their operations. She is especially interested in focusing on news regarding small business startups, hot careers, and internal corporate restructuring for indicators of current business trends.

Starting Point
http://www.stpt.com/magazine/magazine.html
Use the PowerSearch Magazine tool to search magazines found on the Web.

Entrepreneur Magazine
http://www.entrepreneur.mag.com
Features the latest trends and opportunities on U.S.-based small business ventures, and an online version of Entrepreneur International Magazine.

Money Magazine
http://www.moneymag.com
Rates America's 50 hottest jobs (http://pathfinder.com). The best jobs in five Categories (http://pathfinder.com) shows that management consulting ranks high for the money and the security in America.

Asia Week
http://www.asiaweek.com
Check out (http://www.asiaweek.com/Asiaweek/current/issue/newsmap.html), the Asia Newsmap, for news in Singapore, Japan, and beyond.

Fast Company
http://www.fastcompany.com
Reports on change and innovation in the American workplace. An excellent article in the print version on how to globalize your career.

Corporate Web sites

Theresa searches for company listings in management consulting and professional services. She visits the Web sites of the larger firms to establish a benchmark of what is going on in the industry nationally. She wants to zero in on press releases and representative client projects profiled at corporate Web sites.

EDGAR Database of Corporate Information
http://www.sec.gov/edgarhp.htm
A financial database sponsored by the U.S. Securities and Exchange Commission (http://www.sec.gov/index.html).

CompanyLink
http://www.companylink.com/companylookup.cfm
Search by company name or industry for more than 45,000 U.S. companies that are cross-indexed to newswires and press releases.

Booz, Allen & Hamilton
http://www.bah.com
An international management and technology consulting firm.

Price Waterhouse
http://careers.pw-gateway.com/nsCS01HTM
A major U.S. management consulting firm.

Next Steps

Here are some points to consider as you conduct your own online job search:

- Be sure to keep good notes of your online search results. Make note of the URLs; articles; job listings.
- Take notes of important items you find in press releases that you want to investigate further. Print out the job listings that interest you, and use that information to update your resume and prepare for your interviews.
- To avoid unnecessary stops and starts along your virtual job searching commute, take the time to "fill up" on planning strategies and searching skills before starting your trip.
- Be sure that you are familiar with basic Internet skills such as finding and using search engines, sending and receiving email, and navigating with your Web browser.

Chapter 3

Applying for Jobs Online

"It worked...my resume was posted...I have gotten several calls and finally an offer and a job...." This is an actual reply from a job-seeker using an online career and employment resource to find his next job.

Success stories such as this one are exciting indeed. But for others, I have encountered the following comments e-mailed to me from my eResumes & Resources Web site: "I posted my resume on the Internet and haven't received any 'hits' at all!" "I received an e-mail reply from a potential employer who said my resume was 'unreadable.'"

One job-seeker who was getting no responses realized that he was consistently posting his resume in an incompatible file format. His submissions were likely being deleted because they were unreadable to the people viewing them.

Communicating online is very different from communicating on paper. The medium for sending and receiving resumes has certainly changed. What hasn't changed, though, is the purpose of a resume—which is to market skills and abilities in a way that results in interviews.

Traditional paper resumes focus on visual aesthetics and content set off by many action verbs. The goal is to capture attention. Online, a resume must grab a computer's attention by conforming to some electronic standards. Getting noticed today requires an understanding of what those electronic situations are.

Once you understand the new resume "aesthetic," you'll discover the advantages of submitting resumes online. You can get your resume under the nose of the prospective employer—without his or her willing acceptance. The electronic resume is just as valuable as face-to-face networking for uncovering job leads in that it can be electronically stored and retrieved later from anywhere, and at any time. Used in conjunction with face-to-face interviews, the e-resume proves to be invaluable.

Posting resumes online

Chances are, you will post your resume for computer audiences one of three ways: You will send it via e-mail, you will send it via an electronic form (e-form), or you will create a Web page.

Posting your resume on the Internet is analogous to posting a "Ben Hogan golf clubs for sale" flier on a bulletin board where the public can see it. A resume posted on the Internet is usually stored into a database, where thousands of employers and recruiters can retrieve it, and view your qualifications. How do you decide which job posting service to use? Test several services. Results vary by software and technology used. This book will help you understand the key distinctions of each resume-posting method.

With the three posting methods, you'd think that all you have to do is create a resume and randomly post it to many Web sites. But random resume posting will probably produce the same results as mass-mailed resumes—nothing. Targeting the right audiences for making your skills known will affect how your resume is retrieved when recruiters and employers are searching. The challenge in posting is that you never really have an idea who will view your resume, and in what condition it will arrive—if at all. All you know is whether it generated any interviews. To overcome this problem, pay attention to preparing your resume based on the method you choose for posting it in a way that maximizes your chances for getting noticed. By the way, there are certain "controls" that you can implement to monitor the success of your resume once it has been posted. These "controls" will be discussed in later chapters.

The resources in Appendix A list several job boards where you can post your resume. In all cases, where you decide to post your resume will determine how you will prepare it.

The following are some issues to think about when determining which posting method and corresponding type of electronic resume will best suit your needs. You may want to consider preparing a resume that is compatible for each kind of method used to post it.

Electronic mail

If you post your resume via e-mail, you should have a basic understanding of how e-mail works, where to go to get an e-mail account, and how to create a plain-text version of your resume. You should also be able to use attachments, incorporate a cover letter, and take advantage of newer e-mail features such as using hyperlinks and creating an e-mail signature.

Job boards usually require that you submit your resume via e-mail. This is considered *passive* posting—you submit your resume and wait for a response.

Many recruiters like receiving resumes via e-mail because the plain-text format is universal. And for this reason, many recruiters prefer that the resume be in the body of the e-mail message rather than as an e-mail attachment. Chapter 6 will go into more detail on this.

Although e-mail is faster than traditional postal mail, there are delays in delivery. I have sent messages that didn't arrive at their destination until two days later. Also, recruiters note that the absence of contact information in the body of an e-mail message (resume) has prevented them from making contact because the candidate submitted the resume and contact information as an unusable attachment.

Electronic forms

If you are required to complete an e-form when submitting your resume, you will not only have to create an ASCII text-only version of your resume, but you will also need to understand what it means to "copy and paste" text into a form field, how Web-based e-forms work, what information to leave out for privacy reasons, and how to take advantage of job agents to supplement your job search.

The advantage of e-forms over e-mail is that you know exactly what to include on your resume before posting it. You no longer have to debate over whether to include a keyword summary, an objective statement, or bullets. You can also research and organize the information to include in your resume ahead of time before you complete the form.

If you follow the keyword resume tutorial in Chapter 5, you will already have your resume organized so that you can simply copy and paste the appropriate chunks of information needed to complete the e-form. Chapter 7 addresses several frequently-asked questions regarding how to post your resume via an e-form.

Personal Web pages

If you want to create a personal Web page that serves as your resume, you will need to create your resume in HTML. This requires an understanding of basic Web page design principles, HTML, the tools to create Web pages, how to transfer your page onto the Web, and how to monitor its effectiveness once it has been posted (published) onto the Web.

If you are a consultant, publisher, attorney, or freelance graphic artist, a Web resume may be just the thing for you. They are most effective when used in combination with other self-marketing tools in a coordinated job-search campaign. Web resumes are also ideal for people who have high-demand skills, are contingent workers, or have home-based businesses.

Because of the selective nature of the Web, the challenge with Web resumes is getting people to find you. Unlike Web-based resume databases that attract the attention of employers and recruiters by promoting their large databases, job-seekers using Web resumes must attract the attention of interested employers and recruiters on their own.

Chapters 8, 9, and 10 will provide comprehensive coverage on creating and posting a Web resume.

A word about scannable resumes

For employers, scanning is just one way of getting data into a database. Because the Internet is still a growing medium, it may be possible that your e-mailed resume may be printed and then scanned as a separate step in the online application process. However, many employers are finding that scanning is imperfect, because data is easily lost in the process. Resumes sometimes contain many errors because the OCR (Optical Character Recognition) software used to scan them failed to recognize many letters, and are usually discarded.

According to Sandra Grabczynski, the Director of Employer Development at the CareerSite Corporation (http://www.careersite.com), if resumes aren't interpreted correctly when they are scanned, job seekers unknowingly are not included in a company's database.

Current versions of resume database applications such as Restrac will take existing e-mailed resumes and dump them directly into an automated tracking system, bypassing the scanning step. Microsoft, for example, recently discontinued scanning resumes. They now save resumes that are e-mailed to them, convert them to text files, and dump them into a resume database by Restrac. Microsoft doesn't even accept fax copies of resumes in most cases, because the data is too often unusable. They used to accept resumes via e-mail, which were then printed and scanned into a database that is distributed to the recruiters.

Although companies like Microsoft are upgrading their automated resume tracking systems to automatically transfer electronic resume files directly into a database without scanning, many other companies still print and scan their resumes.

A scannable resume emphasizes distinctive edges and recognizable characters. Text is becoming the defacto method for creating a "universal" resume that is compatible across different computer systems.

Defining today's effective resume

There is no perfect way to create the perfect resume. There are some guidelines to follow, however, on what makes it effective—that is, your resume:

- Aligns your career objective to meet the needs of the job market.
- Presents your qualifications to show the kinds of problems you can solve and shows examples of the problems you have solved.
- Incorporates formats that are computer-friendly.
- Answers the "Who," "What," and "So What" within the first 10- to 30-second visual scan.

Jeffrey Banks of Microsoft offers this advice:

"I would encourage candidates applying to Microsoft to think about who they are applying to, if they can't send a Word document, text documents are the next best thing. I would have to question a candidate's fit for the company if they cannot communicate with me electronically."

Take the time to find out what the submission requirements are before submitting your resume electronically. If you aren't exactly sure how you should submit your resume, ask—don't guess. Several online employer and resume posting sites provide specific instructions on how to submit your resume. Test your resume before posting. Send your resume to a friend, colleague, or resume service before actually posting it. Ask them to critique it for you, and ask them to comment on how it looked when they received it. When testing your resume, send yourself a copy so you can see it too. Keep notes on what browsers, word processors, and e-mail programs were used, how the file was sent, and what worked and didn't work.

Online resume services, in particular, are a good resource in several ways. They come in handy if you don't have access to the Internet. They can provide valuable critiques of your resume based on their professional experience, and provide you with additional resource information on where to post your resume. Refer to Appendix B for a listing of several resume writing and posting services.

Rather than try to second guess every single circumstance, consult the source where the resume will be submitted. My general rule is to tailor electronic format based on resume submission requirements, just as you would tailor the content of a cover letter for a specific job your client is applying for.

Chapter 4

A Lesson on File Format

A job-seeker may not have control over *landing* the job, but he or she does have control over creating, preparing, and submitting a resume to a prospective employer. A basic understanding of the new rules required to post an electronic resume on the Internet will maximize job-search success. The new technology poses unique—but not insurmountable challenges—to the job-seeker. For example, sending a resume electronically requires you to create and submit the resume in a way that will be readable to other computers or software. Knowing how you are going to submit your resume *online* will determine how you will prepare your resume *offline*. In this chapter, we'll define and explore file formats and their relationship to electronic resumes.

Identifying the format of a file

The Internet transfers, stores, and retrieves data in units known as files. A file is a complete named collection of information such as a program, a set of data used by a program, or a user-created document. There are many different types of files and to successfully participate on the Internet, both people and computer programs must be familiar with a few common types. File types are distinguished by their "format."

The file formats used today on the Internet are for text, graphics, video, and audio. By convention, files normally have a two- to four-letter extension (typically three) at the end of their filenames (set off by a period). These extensions can identify the kinds of computers compatible for handling and transferring these files. They also identify what computer program(s) may have been used to create and post the resume. This makes it easier to open the file with the appropriate application software. The file formats listed in Figure 1 are some—but not all—of the most commonly used on the Internet.

However, not all files have extensions. Even when files do have extensions, they don't always reflect the type of data in the file. With the Macintosh, extensions rarely make a difference in the way the operating system deals with files. However, this can cause problems in the Windows environment. File types are registered by extension, so filenames without extensions, or with extensions that aren't registered with the Windows software on the recipient's computer, can be difficult to work with. This issue comes up frequently when transferring files over e-mail. Some older e-mail programs and systems do not preserve attachment filenames. Besides, users receiving messages with mangled or missing filenames are left to figure out what type of file the attachment is. Sending resumes over e-mail as attachments is discussed in further detail in Chapter 6.

.au	Most common sound format found on the Web. Binary. Sound Player (http://wwwhost.ots.utexas.edu/mac/pub-mac-sound.html) is a multipurpose sound program that can record and playback this file format.
.bin	Macbinary II Encoded File. Download as MacBinary or Binary. Commonly used in Apple Macintosh computers.
.doc	Microsoft Word file format that can be viewed on the Web using Word View (http://www.microsoft.com) to quickly display (not edit) Word documents without having to launch the Microsoft Word application.
.exe	Executable file. One popular use of this format on the Internet is as self-extracting files in DOS/Windows that can be downloaded and launched in a temporary directory.
.gif	Graphical Interchange Format, a very common graphics format used on the Internet. Use GIF Converter (http://www.kamit.com/gifconverter.html) or JPEGView (http://www.macworld.com/software/Software.832.html) for viewing and converting between GIF, PICT, TIFF, and JPG file formats. This format is viewable in a Web browser.
.html/.htm	Hypertext Markup Language, a plain-text file format used to create Web pages. Use either Microsoft Internet Explorer or Netscape Communicator browsers to view the file.
.hqx	BinHex 4.0, a common MAC OS file format used to transfer files on the Internet. Use Stuffit Expander (www.aladdinsys.com) to decompress this file.
.jpg/.jpeg	Joint Photographic Experts Group, a common graphics format used on the Web. Use GIF Converter (http://www.kamit.com/gifconverter.html) or JPEGView (http://www.macworld.com/software/Software.832.html) to view and convert GIF, PICT, TIFF, and JPG file formats. This format is viewable in a Web browser.
.mpg/.mpeg	MPEG is the standard movie file format used on the Internet. Most newer computers shipped today include drivers than can play these files.
.mov	QuickTime Movie, a native Mac OS video file format. Use QuickTime (http://quicktime.apple.com/) to view these files—it is available for either MAC OS or Windows.
.pdf	Adobe Acrobat's Portable Document Format. Documents created in this format can be viewed (not edited) using Adobe's freely available Acrobat Reader.
.sea	MAC OS self extracting file format.
.tiff	A very large, high-quality image format that has to be converted to GIF or JPG before you can upload and view the file onto the Web. Or, you can use JPEG View (http://www.macworld.com/software/Software.832.html) to view the picture as it is.
.txt	A plain-text file commonly used in the body of electronic mail messages.
.wav	Windows Wave sound file format. Use SoundApp for MAC OS or Windows to play this file.
.zip	Pkzip, a common DOS/Windows compression format. Use WinZip for Windows or Stuffit Expander for Mac OS to decompress this file.

Figure 1. Commonly Used Internet File Formats.

Transferring files

File formats exist so that applications can store and retrieve data electronically. Files are the fundamental way that data is transferred from program to program and computer system to computer system. The most familiar purpose of a file is to save the work you've done. A file consists of data, and different file formats give file data different degrees of *portability*. This "getting around" occurs in many ways, such as on a floppy disk, through networks, and over modems.

File formats also give file data different degrees of *richness* in terms of the kind of information and how it is presented. Unfortunately, richness and portability often oppose each other and you have to make trade-offs when deciding on the format to use. To understand how a text-based file format is used to transfer your electronic resume, some information about how computers and the Internet work will help:

ASCII file formats

Computers can process numbers in many different ways, and can similarly process text that has been converted to numbers. Each character on your computer keyboard is stored according to a universally standardized code that assigns a number to each letter, numeric figure, punctuation mark, and symbol. This code is called ASCII (pronounced (ASK-ee), which stands for the American Standard Code for Information Interchange.

Text files are the most common type of data files found on the Internet. Although they seem very simple at first, there is one drawback: There is no text formatting— meaning the text within the file format does not include common elements such as underlining, bold-face characters, italics, and other type variances.

Another complicating factor is that text alone is increasingly inadequate. People want to augment their printed documents with graphics, charts, footnotes, headers, and fonts. Online documents may need to contain animation, links to networked databases, and audio annotations. When you combine these different ways of presenting information, you have what is known as multimedia documents.

Formats for online communication must be easily manipulated on a wide variety of systems (high portability). For electronic resumes, there are three popular file formats all coded in ASCII: plain-text, rich-text, and hypertext. By reasonably assessing what electronic methods you will be asked to submit your resume (in terms of e-mail systems and word processors) used by both the sender and recipient, you can prepare your resume in the appropriate file format.

Plain-text (.txt)

ASCII text-only files are recognized universally. They contain characters, spaces, punctuation, carriage returns, and sometimes tabs. The benefit of an ASCII plain-text resume is that it can be read by PCs, Macintoshes, UNIX Workstations, or mainframe terminals. Unfortunately, ASCII plain-text files are exactly what they sound like—plain. A plain-text file doesn't have fonts, embedded graphics, headings, titles, footnotes, italics, or other features that would help to make the text more attractive and easier to understand. This limitation means that resumes submitted over the Internet must consist of plain-text with no formatting, which is something to get used to when traditional resume-writing advice has evangelized the use of varied fonts and effective text formatting designs.

Rich-text (.rtf)

Most job-seekers are used to creating their resumes in a word processor, which does provide the fancy formatting options. The ASCII rich-text-file format, identified by the `.rtf` file extension, is popular because of its compatibility with word processors. Whenever you anticipate sending your resume as an e-mail attachment in the original form that you created in a word processor, you should get in the habit of saving it as a rich-text file.

The ASCII rich-text-file format can be viewed by popular word processors such as Corel WordPerfect and Microsoft Word while retaining the character, paragraph and page formatting, as well as the overall physical appearance of the formatted hard-copy version. Most word processors and desktop publishing programs use this approach to give users the ability to save portable versions of their documents.

However, the destination computer may not recognize a rich-text file. In addition, rich-text is not commonly supported by e-mail editors, thus sending such a file in the body of an e-mail message will result in unreadable text. Some e-mail programs (such as Microsoft Outlook) implement rich-text by placing the formatting information into a hidden attachment. However, most older e-mail programs don't support attachments and end up putting this coding data into the body of the message, making it potentially unreadable. If you are not sure what e-mail system and e-mail desktop program your recipient is using, it's best to avoid rich-text.

Hypertext (.html)

Hypertext is also an ASCII file format, identified by its `.htm` or `.html` file extension. HTML (Hypertext Markup Language) uses a feature called "markup" to provided added flexibility in formatting your electronic resume.

In word processors, "markup" refers to the exact appearance of a piece of text. For example, "centered in 14 pt bold Times New Roman" text commands are used, and the entire word-processed document is processed to generate an output that contains this physical markup.

On the Web, markup of text is important to the exchange of electronic documents. When using hypertext, HTML marks up the text in a way that makes a piece of text significant. The way to preserve markup for Web pages is to include markup information in the text. Hypertext provides an overall framework to create pages rich in text, graphics, sounds, animations, and other forms of data.

HTML itself is widely misunderstood. Many HTML documents on the Web contain detailed formatting commands that allow the document to look very nice on a particular browser on a particular operating system—and on a particular size of computer screen. But HTML does not allow you to control the total appearance of a document. Rather, HTML allows you to suggest how the document should be displayed in your Web browser.

Different browsers can (and should) interpret those suggestions in different ways. For example, under the **View** menu on Internet Explorer, you can configure your browser to view Web pages with a specific font with a specific font size. You will learn more about this when building your own Web resume in Chapters 8, 9, and 10.

GIF and JPEG files

The two most common graphic file formats used on the Web are:

- **GIF** (Graphic Interchange Format), identified by the .gif file extension.
- **JPEG** (Joint Photographic Experts Group), identified by the .jpg file extension.

Both file formats are bitmaps (dot by dot, or pixel by pixel). Because bitmaps tend to be very large image files, file compression is needed to reduce file size and download time. The .gif and .jpeg formats provide file compression. Convert images to either of these formats before using them in a Web page.

In general, .gif is best for small images, line drawings, and images with areas of solid colors, where data loss becomes more obvious. The .jpeg format is best for photographs with gradual shading, where data loss is less noticeable. It is also commonly used for background images.

The .gif format provides other benefits. The .gif format can make one color transparent—hence the image appears to "float" over or blend into a background color or image. Pictures in the .gif format can also be used for simple Web animations.

Choosing the right file format

Before submitting your resume electronically, find out about the submission requirements. Several online employer and resume posting sites provide specific instructions on how to submit your resume. Send your resume to a friend, colleague, or resume service before actually posting it on the Internet. Send a copy to yourself so you can see the final product. Keep notes on what browsers, word processors, and e-mail programs were used in its creation; on what way the resume file was sent (e-form, e-mail, and so forth); and what worked—and didn't work.

As a general rule of thumb, think in terms of these three guidelines to help you determine how to format your resume:

1. If you transmit your resume via e-mail, its file is stored on your PC and viewed with your e-mail reader. The most common file format used is ASCII plain-text.

2. If you transmit your resume via electronic form, once you hit the submit button after completing the form, your resume file is stored in a database, and viewed by the database's software interface. Data transmitted via forms are, in most cases, converted to ASCII plain-text. Electronic forms will be discussed in more detail in Chapter 7.

3. If you transmit your resume with the Hypertext Transfer Protocol (HTTP), its file is stored on a Web server, and viewed by a Web browser. The file format it is transmitted in is ASCII hypertext. HTTP itself is used to transfer and retrieve Web documents. Referring again to the pizzeria example in Chapter 1: In order for the cook to continue making pizza, he needs to order the ingredients on a regular basis. The way a cook would use the phone to order and receive those ingredients is similar to what HTTP does in transferring and receiving files.

File compression

Compressing a file is like compacting trash in a trash compactor in order to save space. Each file takes up an amount of disk and memory space on a computer. To conserve this space in order to save transfer time or store within restricted limits, you can compress files, which shrinks the amount of space a file takes up.

There are many utilities out on the Internet that you can use to compress your files. These are especially useful when you are sending large files via e-mail. File compression will become a must if you eventually create a web site—you'll need such a utility to transfer all of your files to a host.

Care must be taken when selecting a file compression utility, though. Different utilities may produce different formats, and you want to use a utility that uses a common format so that the recipient of the compressed file can successfully decompress it. When sending compressed files, the steps are:

- Create your file(s).
- Run the compression utility to produce the compressed file.
- Attach the compressed file to an e-mail message and transfer the file.

My advice is to avoid sending your resume as a compressed file, unless you are specified to do so. Most e-mail programs will support a maximum file size of 1.0 to 1.5 MB, which is plenty of space for a plain-text resume. The only time you may need to zip a resume is when graphics or pictures are included.

For compression utilities, try Shareware.com (http://www.shareware.com) or Download.com (http://www.download.com) to download these utilities.

Probably the most popular compression utility for the PC is WinZip 6.3. It compresses files in the .zip format, the most popular compressed file format. WinZip is a straightforward zipping and unzipping utility that includes built-in support for popular Internet file formats. WinZip also includes an interface to the Internet

Browser Support add-on, which lets you download and open `.zip` files from the Internet with one click via Internet Explorer or Netscape Navigator. This compression utility is available for Microsoft Windows 95 and Microsoft Windows NT operating systems.

A popular compression utility for MAC OS is StuffIt Expander 4.5. This utility compresses and decompresses just about any file. This compression utility is available for MAC OS operating system. You can obtain it, along with many other MAC OS files at `www.macdownload.com`.

Chapter 5

Writing Resumes for the Internet

As more and more employers ask that you apply for jobs online, it makes sense to know how to write resumes for the Internet. Content is still king when it comes to resume development. In this chapter, you will learn how to create your master keyword resume that captures your skills and abilities in terms of keywords and chunks of information that will become useful in posting your resume online for a variety of situations.

Nouns are the "keywords" that employers look for in screening potential candidates. Keywords are used to search for, index, and retrieve your electronic resume. Your resume should contain many keywords, which are nouns and phrases that highlight technical and professional areas of expertise, industry-related jargon, projects, achievements, special task forces and other distinctive features about your work history. The advantage of keywords is that they provide the context from which to search for a resume in a database. They also give human viewers the opportunity to assess skills and qualifications at a glance when using a Web resume or paper resume. There is a high probability that your ink-on-paper resume will be transformed into electronic data and entered into databases. This means your resume must also incorporate formats that are computer-friendly, which requires a basic understanding of the data retrieval process and a new approach to the way you write your resume that makes it flexible enough to take advantage of that process.

Using keywords for easy data retrieval

It is content, not technology, that is common to all forms of electronic resumes, regardless of their file format. But it is database technology that makes your content stand out in a digital age. A database is a way to store and organize data that is alike in some way. Internet databases where you can store your resume come in several forms. The three most popular ways of gathering information are newsgroups via e-mail; job boards via e-mail and e-forms; and search engines via submitting a Web page's Internet address.

When resumes are scanned or downloaded, the data from them are placed into a database for later retrieval. Employers and recruiters routinely search through resume databases using keywords. Remember that keywords should be pertinent to your career, and should contain terms, projects, areas of knowledge related to your field of work. These resume databases will need these keywords in order to select the right person for the job—and it might as well be you! Your goal is to have the right keywords in your resume so you end up on their "hit list."

A recruiter's search query can be formulated in three different ways:

- One or more keywords. Documents containing the specified keywords are retrieved and displayed to the user.
- Multiple keywords in a Boolean search. A Boolean search is a query that uses the Boolean operators **AND, OR**, and **NOT** to create keyword relationships that include or exclude documents during a search operation. You may use the Boolean operators AND, OR and NOT to combine words and phrases. These operators can be typed in lower-case or upper-case letters depending on the database you use. In the Alta Vista search engine (http://www.altavista.com), for example, let's say a recruiter types in the following: "resume AND (programmer OR developer)." This search query indicates that he or she is searching for documents that contain the keyword "resume" in it, and that he or she also wants those documents, or resumes, to include either the word "programmer" or "developer."
- Natural language request that is converted into Boolean. For example, the natural language request in the HotBot (http://www.hotbot.com) search engine: Resume programmer developer would interpret this query as a Boolean AND search. In other words, it takes the keywords as you type them naturally and assumes you are looking for documents with all of these words. If you were to use HotBot's "More Search Options" features, you can select "all the words" as described above, or "any of the words." If you choose this latter option, HotBot would interpret your query as a Boolean OR search. In other words, it will assume you are looking for documents with either the words "resume" or "programmer" or "developer."

These are very simplified examples, but they all should give you an idea of the relationship of keywords to searching a database. Keywords are the primary basis of the electronic search and retrieval process. Keywords are tools to quickly browse a resume's text. Keywords are used to identify and retrieve documents for the user. Keywords are the instruments that will sell your electronic resume to an employer.

The emphasis is not on trying to second-guess every possible keyword a recruiter may use to find your resume. Your focus is on selecting and organizing your resume's content in order to highlight those keywords for a variety of online situations. The idea is to identify all possible keywords that are appropriate to your skills and accomplishments that support the kinds of jobs you are looking for, and record them on a "master" keyword list. It is from this list that you can consolidate keywords that repeat themselves and highlight those that support the job objective. But to do that, you must apply traditional resume-writing principles to the concept of extracting those keywords from your resume. Once you have written your resume, then you can identify your strategic keywords based on how you imagine people will search for your resume.

Creating your master resume for paper and electronic use

The first step in creating your electronic resume is to actually write it "the old-fashioned way." By analyzing the resume writing process, you can easily focus on the keywords appropriate to your vocation.

The selection and number of keywords and phrases you choose are completely subjective, depending on your career objective and the type of position you are applying for. The best approach is to create a master resume that captures this information. With a master resume, it is just a matter of revising the content and altering the electronic format of the resume, rather than rewriting the entire resume for every new submission. You can customize your resume with the least amount of effort. You have one master version of your resume that can be reformatted in several ways.

Quick refresher of traditional resume styles

Before you begin creating your online resume, it's best to review the basics of resume writing as it relates to capturing your skills, accomplishments, and keywords first. That way, when you begin formatting your electronic file, the content will be your least concern.

Although there are several variations, the three basic categories of resume styles can also be applied to an electronic resume. These are chronological, functional, and combination.

Chronological resume style

The chronological resume style organizes information by job titles presented in chronological order, usually listing the most current job first. The emphasis is on positions held and the companies where you worked.

Some Advantages:
- Simple and direct.
- Highlights a steady work record.
- Works well in conservative industries, such as banking and health.

Some Disadvantages:
- Format will highlight gaps in your work history.
- Ineffective for new college graduates, or those who have very little work experience.
- Focuses on the past rather than the future.

Functional resume style

The functional resume style organizes information by skills or job functions, usually highlighting those skills and functions of the job being sought.

Some Advantages:
- Works well for career changes (e.g., military) because it presents skills that can be used in other jobs.
- Maximizes experience for job seekers with a minimal work history.
- Useful when highlighting work in previous paying or nonpaying jobs.

Some Disadvantages:
- Can appear suspicious, as if you are hiding something (for example, job hopping or insufficient experience).
- Can appear confusing if not written well.
- Can appear as if you are over-selling yourself because the focus is more on self-marketing and less on work history.

Combination resume style

The combination resume style combines work history and job functions, tied together with a list of career achievements.

Some Advantages:
- Takes advantage of those with successful career records.
- Sells what you do and provides a work history to prove it.
- Good format for those with a long work history.

Some Disadvantages:
- Requires an established work history.
- Requires an established track record of career achievements.
- Requires care in organizing content to avoid confusion.

The elements of your resume

The first step in preparing your master resume is planning its structure. To do this, you will need to gather every crumb of useful information about yourself and your career. These informational elements will clarify your career goals to prospective employers—and to yourself.

The following steps will allow you to create a well-organized resume, complete with a large selection of keywords—a very important commodity for an e-resume. These items are listed in the order they would normally appear on your resume, from the general to the specific. Once your master resume is written, you will be able to concentrate fully on preparing it for the Internet without worrying about its content.

Heading information

The heading information on your resume should contain your name, address, phone numbers, and your e-mail address if you have one.

Objective

An objective specifies your target market and/or job title. It is your call on whether to include an objective. If you use it, one method that has worked extremely well is to state the position that you are applying for. Not only is this brief and to the point, it includes yet another set of important keywords. Your cover letter can elaborate on your career objective further.

Supporters of objectives say that they assist recruiters in identifying what your purpose for applying is. Opponents of it say that your objective is implied based on the specific job you are applying for. Regardless, an objective can provide a focus for organizing your resume's content.

Employment data

Information about past employment is the backbone of any resume. It documents your employment history and provides specific information about the types of jobs you had. Most importantly, it shows how you can fit into a new position. For each job, you should have the following:

- Name of employer.
- Location of employer (city, state).
- Dates employed.
- Job title areas.

Although job titles and employer names will give your resume background, what you did at each job gives your application context. It tells employers about your abilities and how they can be utilized to their benefit. Make sure that you think about these elements when writing your resume:

- Job responsibilities.
- Job skills.
- Job accomplishments.

Job responsibilities

Job responsibilities describe your work duties. This description reflects distinctive tasks that you have performed, or are held accountable for performing.

Job skills

Job skills are specific and unique to your work experience, profession, and career goals. They indicate your level of proficiency in a given area as a result of carrying out your job responsibilities.

Job accomplishments

Job accomplishments answer the "so what" questions as a result of the tasks you performed in your job. They indicate the degree of benefit you provided to your employer as a function of how well you applied the skills you used in performing a specific task.

Formal education and specialized training

Formal education is characterized by the award of an accredited degree or certificate, and includes the following information:

- Degree or certificate earned.
- Name of institution.
- Location of institution (city and state).
- Major area of study; credits earned.
- Date of completion.

Specialized training includes training that was received at seminars, workshops, on-the-job training, and other in-house training programs for which no specific accredited degree or certificate was awarded. However, this training is important to professional development and indicates training that supports your job objective. You should include the following information about your specialized training:

- Name of training received.
- Name of organization that provided the training.
- Date of completion.

Placement of your education and training on your resume only matters if you are submitting a paper hard copy that will not be scanned or entered into a database. Typically, if you have 15 or more years of experience, you can list your education toward the end of the resume. If your education is pertinent to the position you are applying (for example, it requires a master's or doctorate degree), then you would want to list this item before you list your employment history.

Personal data

Personal data includes pertinent awards received, professional memberships, offices held in professional associations, titles of publications authored, etc., if they support your job objective. This section can easily be modified according to your specific job objective.

Keyword elements

The best way to construct the content of your resume and extract its keywords is to start with the highest level of detail in documenting your work experience, and then summarizing this detail for inclusion at the beginning of your resume. Working from specific to general level of detail helps you to assess your skills and accomplishments, refine your career objective, and focus on your resume's keyword content. The primary benefit to integrating keyword elements into your resume is that keywords provide the context from which to retrieve your resume from electronic databases.

You can compile a list of keywords for your industry using a variety of sources. The most readily available sources are the Department of Labor's *Occupational Outlook Handbook* (http://stats.bls.gov/oco/oco1000.htm), the classified ads of newspapers and trade magazines, and actual job announcements found at corporate Web sites.

I usually apply two rules of thumb when determining keyword selection and presentation: Limit the number of keywords to 25 to 35; and prioritize their order the same way you would prioritize the information presented in the resume. Your keywords can be categorized into the following three groups for the purpose of prioritizing them:

- Keyword summaries.
- Skill keywords by job category and function.
- Personal trait keywords.

Make sure that you focus primarily on your accomplishments, rather than just your responsibilities. Your accomplishments will give you the competitive advantage in this results-oriented job market.

Preparing your master resume step by step

The following steps illustrate a systematic approach to squeezing keywords while developing a resume. You can integrate any of the following steps into your own resume development process:

STEP 1:   Clarify your job objective.
STEP 2:   List each of your job/position titles in chronological order.
STEP 3:   List your responsibilities for each job held.
STEP 4:   List the skills you used for each job.
STEP 5:   List your accomplishments that illustrate each skill used.
STEP 6:   Write a statement qualifying or quantifying each accomplishment.
STEP 7:   List your specialized training and education.
STEP 8:   Extract important keywords and summarize.
STEP 9:   Summarize your qualifications relevant to your job objective.
STEP 10: Write the actual resume text.

Each step is presented in a logical order that your resume should be developed in. Later steps will be completed with the information from the earlier steps.

Follow each step for each employment position held. The following exercise is based on the current employment position held for the resume template found in Appendix A.

Step 1: Clarify your job objective

Your final resume may or may not contain an objective statement, depending upon the resume bank you post your resume to. However, it's important to develop your resume with a clear objective in mind so that you know how to organize and prioritize your resume's content.

To get a grip on your objective, apply a systematic "brainstorming" approach:

First, make a list of all of the job titles you can think of that describe the kinds of work you want to do in your next job (e.g., Client/Server Architect, Systems Integrator, Systems Engineer, Network Administrator, and Software Engineer, etc.).

Second, make a list of all of the workplaces you can think of that might hire people for those kinds of jobs. For example, list specific employers (e.g., Netscape Communications, Microsoft Corporation, Sun Microsystems, Oracle, etc.) or general descriptions of work places (e.g., high-technology firm, small start-up company, etc.)

Third, organize your job title list and workplaces list into three groups each: first priority now, second priority later, and third priority maybe later.

Finally, match up the first priority job titles with the first priority workplaces, and you have the beginning of an objective statement. For example, let's say Client/Server Architect and Systems Integrator are your first priority job titles, and a major high-technology firm is your first priority workplace. Your objective statement would then read three ways:

Job Objective 1:
"Position as a Client/Server Systems Architect for a major high-technology firm."
Job Objective 2:
"Position as a Client/Server Architect for a major high-technology firm that specializes in systems integration."
Job Objective 3:
"Position as a Client/Server Architect for Sun Microsystems."

With these objective statements, you can prioritize and organize the information you need to include in your resume that supports this objective: for example, your computer skills; education, including continuing education in computer science; systems integration experience; technical consulting skills; and certifications.

EXAMPLE:

For the purpose of this tutorial, we'll select the first job objective:
"Position as a Client Server Systems Architect for a major high-technology firm."

Step 2: List each of your job/position titles in chronological order

Make a list of each position or job title you have had, whether it was paid or nonpaid. For each listed item, include the following information:

- Position or job title.
- Company/organization name.
- Department/division.
- Location (city and state).
- Dates employed.

EXAMPLE:

Position or job title: systems engineer

Employment data:

- Company/organization name: Science Applications International Corporation (SAIC).
- Department/division: Systems Integration Division.
- Location: McLean, Virginia
- Dates employed: 1996–Present.

Step 3: List your responsibilities for each job held

Your job responsibilities are synonymous with a job description. A good source of example job descriptions are from the jobs advertised online by individual employers. They are unique identifiers that define the nature of your work relative to your accountability to accomplish specific work tasks.

EXAMPLE:

Job description: "Provide systems engineering, software engineering, technical consulting, and marketing services as a member of the Systems Integration Division of a software consulting company."

Job responsibilities:

- Provide systems and software engineering.
- Provide technical consulting.
- Provide marketing services.

Step 4: List the skills you used for each job

Skills highlight your abilities, expertise, proficiency, and understanding of key areas that you develop as a result of your work experience and education.

List the specific skills that are unique to your work experience, profession, and career goals. This list of skills will serve two purposes: to generate a list of accomplishments using these skills, and to develop your keyword summary.

EXAMPLE:

Job skills used as a systems engineer:

- Knowledge of client/server architecture, Windows for Workgroups, Windows NT Advanced Server, Microsoft SQL Server, Oracle7, and UNIX; knowledge of SMP, RDBMS, and RAID technology.
- Project management and development skills.
- Software and systems planning and design skills.
- Technical specification and presentation skills, interpersonal skills, troubleshooting skills, and consulting skills.
- Technology analysis and integration skills, business management skills, and marketing skills.

Step 5: List your accomplishments that illustrate each skill used

By definition, accomplishments are tasks that you successfully completed as a result of using a particular set of skills that were required for a particular job. A better way to think of this is something you completed for the benefit of your employer that answers the question, "So what?" These accomplishments should support the skills that you identified in **Step 4**. Describe an accomplishment for each responsibility listed.

EXAMPLE:

The following are examples of a successfully completed task for some of the job responsibilities listed in **Step 4**:

- Prepared and presented preliminary designs to corporate project managers.
- Developed an enterprise-level client/server automated auditing application.
- Conducted trade studies of leading-edge technologies consistent with internal performance standards.

Step 6: Write a specific statement that quantifies each accomplishment

Qualifying or quantifying your accomplishments indicates to *what degree* a task was completed successfully that you identified in **Step 5**. These statements should address "how much and how efficiently."

EXAMPLE:

The following are examples of a specific statement that indicates the degree to which each accomplishment listed in **STEP 5** was successfully completed:

- Selected as the Systems Engineering Lead on a Federal agency terabyte database modernization project. This project succeeded in migrating from mainframe to client/server technology.
- Designed and managed the development of an enterprise-level client/server automated auditing application for the cost management division of a major

long-distance telephone service provider. Migrated from mainframe computers, db2, and FOCUS to workgroup-oriented, client/server architecture involving Windows for Workgroups, Windows NT Server, Microsoft SQL Server, Oracle7, and UNIX.
- Conducted extensive trade studies of a large number of vendors that offered leading-edge technologies; these studies identified proven (low-risk) implementations of symmetric multiprocessing computers (SMP) and Relational Database Management Systems (RDBMS) that met stringent performance and availability criteria.

Step 7: List education, certifications, and specialized training

When listing your formal education, you should include the following information in your list:

- Degree or certificate earned.
- Name of institution.
- Location of institution (city and state).
- Major area of study; credits earned if incomplete.
- Date of or expected date of completion.

EXAMPLE:

- BS, Mathematics and Computer Science, University of California, Los Angeles, 1990; GPA 3.57.
- Microsoft Certified Systems Engineer (MCSE #132546), August, 1997. (List your certifications by type, certification number, and date obtained).
- Microsoft Certified Product Specialist, TCP/IP Networking, June, 1997.

Your specialized training includes other relevant on-the-job work experience or training that illustrates your professional development. If you've taken certification classes, try not to list every class you've ever taken. Instead, list classes completed within the past two years, and special training that sets you apart from your peers. When listing your specialized training, you should include the following information in your list:

- Name of training received.
- Name of organization or department that provided the training.
- Date of completion.

EXAMPLE:

- Transmission Control Protocol/Internet Protocol (TCP/IP), Technology Systems Institute, 1996.
- Database Administration, Performance Tuning, and Benchmarking with Oracle7, Oracle Corporation, 1995.

- Computer Systems Technology Program, Air Force Institute of Technology (AFIT), Graduate Courses in Software Engineering and Computer Communications (24 quarter units completed), 1992.

Step 8: Extract important keywords and summarize

Take a look at the keywords generated so far in Steps 1 through 7 and highlight those nouns you think that someone might use as keywords to find your resume. Ask yourself whether those keywords adequately describe your work experience and support your job objectives.

Keyword summaries are also useful when developing a Web resume and traditional paper resume. They not only attract search engines that index Web resumes by keywords, but they also provide a human viewer the opportunity to assess your skills and qualifications at a glance.

The keyword summary that you develop for each one of your jobs will be kept in your master keyword list. From these, you will develop a master keyword summary for your resume, consolidating those keywords that overlap, and the ones that are applicable to the particular job that you are applying for. The master keyword summary will include various keywords from your education, specialized training, and personal data sections, as well. See Appendix C for strategies on creating keyword summaries.

In the following example, a client/server architect might consider including the keywords in the following order: hardware, network hardware, network operating systems, protocols, desktop operating systems, languages, applications, miscellaneous for skills and technical proficiencies.

Extract the important keywords for this job held. You would create a keyword summary for every job you've held by extracting the important keywords as follows:

- **Job title**: Systems Engineer.
- **Job responsibilities**: Systems Analysis. Systems Integration. Technical Consulting. Marketing.
- **Job accomplishments**: Enterprise-level client/server applications. Preliminary design. Trade studies. Mainframe to client/server system migration. New technology integration.
- **Job skills**: Knowledge of client/server architecture. Windows for Workgroups. Windows NT Advanced Server. Microsoft SQL Server. Oracle7 and UNIX. Knowledge of SMP, RDBMS, and RAID technology. Project Management and Development skills. Software and Systems Planning and Design skills. Technical specification and presentation skills. Interpersonal, troubleshooting, and consulting skills. Technology analysis and integration skills. Business management skills. Marketing skills.
- **Industry-related jargon, buzzwords, acronyms, etc.**: SMP. RDBMS. UNIX. TCP/IP. BETA Tester. Windows NT. Troubleshooting. Client/Server Architecture.

- **Keyword Summary for a Systems Engineer:** Systems Engineer. Systems Analysis. Systems Integration. Enterprise-level Client/Server Applications. Preliminary Design. Trade Studies. Mainframe to Client/Server System Migration. New Technology Integration. Windows for Workgroups. Windows NT Advanced Server. Project Management and Development skills. Software and Systems Planning and Design skills. Technology Analysis and Integration skills. Business Management and Marketing skills.
- **Programming Languages:** C. C++. Visual BASIC. FORTRAN. Pascal. SQL. OSF/Motif. UNIX Shell Script (sh, ksh, csh). BASIC. Clipper. Algol 68. 80X86 Assembler.
- **Operating Systems:** UNIX (bsd & SVr3/r4). MS Windows. MS DOS. MS Windows NT. Solaris. HP-UX. Ultrix. AIX. VAX/VMS. Mac OS 8.5.
- **Networking:** TCP/IP. OSI. Microsoft LAN Manager. Novell Netware. DDN. Internet. Ethernet. Token Ring. SNA. X.25. LAN-WAN interconnection.
- **Applications:** Microsoft Office. Microsoft Access. Microsoft Visual C++. Microsoft Project. Microsoft Publisher. Lotus 123. Lotus Freelance. System Architect.

Step 9: Summarize your qualifications relevant to your job objective

The summary should be a concise statement highlighting three to five of your achievements in work, areas of expertise, qualifications, technical or professional skills, and any other distinctive qualifications. It is best completed after outlining your skills profile, employment history, and education. It should grab the reader's attention within the first 30 seconds of reading your resume.

EXAMPLE:

Summary of qualifications as an experienced Systems Engineer:

- **Number of years in this position**: Three years.
- **Relevant credentials, training, and/or education**: BS in Computer Science; Performance Tuning with Oracle7; Software Engineering Management Training.
- **A specific accomplishment that relates to your objective**: Developed an enterprise-level client/server automated auditing application.
- **A quality or personal trait that supports your objective**: Successfully migrated a financial management company from a mainframe computer system to a client/server system.
- **Another accomplishment or trait that supports your objective**: Technical consulting, business management, and marketing skills.

Step 10: Write the actual resume text

The keyword element is incorporated into either the chronological, functional, or combination resume style formats. For this tutorial, the combination style was used.

EXAMPLE:

Content organization for Thomas B. Seeker's master keyword resume:

- Objective.
- Keyword Summary.
- Qualifications Summary.
- Technical Skills.
- Professional Experience.
- Other Work Experience.
- Education.
- Specialized Training.
- Special Honors and Professional Affiliations.

Summary (Steps 1-10)

The value of a master resume is to help you organize and compartmentalize your resume's information prior to posting it online. It's better to revise part of something rather than redo the entire thing. Let's summarize steps 1-10 and see what we have:

1. Job objective:
Client/Server Systems Architect for a major high-technology firm.

2. Current job title and employment data:
- Position or job title: systems engineer.
- Company/organization name: Science Applications International Corporation (SAIC).
- Department/division: Systems Integration Division.
- Location: McLean, Virginia
- Dates employed: 1996–Present.

3. Job Responsibilities:
- Provide systems and software engineering.
- Provide technical consulting.
- Provide marketing services.

4. Job Skills:
- Knowledge of client/server architecture, Windows for Workgroups, Windows NT Advanced Server, Microsoft SQL Server, Oracle7 and UNIX; knowledge of SMP, RDBMS, and RAID technology.
- Project management and development skills.
- Software and systems planning and design skills.
- Technical specification and presentation skills, interpersonal skills, troubleshooting skills, and consulting skills.
- Technology analysis and integration skills, business management skills, and marketing skills.

5. Job Accomplishments:

- Developed an enterprise-level client/server automated auditing application.
- Prepared and presented preliminary designs to corporate project managers.
- Conducted trade studies of leading-edge technologies consistent with internal performance standards.

6. Job Accomplishments Qualified/Quantified:

- Designed and managed the development of an enterprise-level client/server automated auditing application for the cost management division of a major long-distance telephone service provider. Migrated from mainframe computers, db2, and FOCUS to workgroup oriented, client/server architecture involving Windows for Workgroups, Windows NT Server, Microsoft SQL Server, Oracle7, and UNIX.
- Selected as the Systems Engineering Lead on a Federal agency terabyte database modernization project. This project succeeded in migrating from mainframe to client/server technology.
- Conducted extensive trade studies of a large number of vendors that offered leading-edge technologies; these studies identified proven (low-risk) implementations of symmetric multiprocessing computers (SMP) and Relational Database Management Systems (RDBMS) that met stringent performance and availability criteria.

7. Education & Specialized Training:

- BS, Mathematics and Computer Science, University of California, Los Angeles, 1990; GPA: 3.57.
- Database Administration, Performance Tuning, and Benchmarking with Oracle7, Oracle Corporation, 1995.
- Software Requirements Engineering and Management Course; Computer Applications International Corporation.

8. Keyword Summary for a Systems Engineer:

Systems Engineer. Systems Analysis. Systems Integration. Client/Server Applications. Preliminary Design. Trade Studies. Mainframe to Client/Server System Migration. New Technology Integration. Windows for Workgroups Windows NT Advanced Server. Project Management and Development skills. Software and Systems Planning and Design skills. Technology Analysis and Integration skills. Business Management and Marketing skills.

9. Qualifications Summary as a Systems Engineer:

Three years of experience in developing, designing, and implementing enterprise-level client/server applications; a proven track record in successful migration from mainframe systems to client/server systems.

The "master" keyword summary will consolidate those keywords that overlap for each of your jobs, and prioritize those keywords that are applicable to the job that you are applying for. It is the master keyword summary that will ultimately be placed at the beginning of your resume, and will include relevant education, specialized training, and personal data relating to the position you are applying for. After completing steps 1 through 10 for each job position you have held, the master keyword summary would appear as follows:

Systems Engineer. Client/Server System Architect. Systems Analysis. Systems Integration. Network Administration. Database Administration. Systems Administration. Software Engineering. Troubleshooting Computing Systems. C++. Visual Basic. SQL. UNIX Shell Script. Windows. MS DOS. Windows NT. TCP/IP. OSI. Microsoft LAN Manager. Novell Netware. Project Management. Trade Studies. Consulting. BETA Tester. Technical Presentations. Sales Presentations. Instructor. BS Degree. Mathematics and Computer Science. UCLA. M.S. Degree. Computer Engineering.

The Keyword Summary can be integrated into the Qualifications Summary; they were separated in this tutorial for illustration purposes in identifying key blocks of information that can be later manipulated to suit a specific need. You can even substitute your traditional Objective statement with the Qualifications Summary.

10. Write actual resume text:

Combining the information obtained from Steps 1-10, the actual written resume text for the Systems Engineer position would looks as follows:

THOMAS B. SEEKER
4120 Bellow Drive, Baltimore, MD 21203
Voice: (410) 422-8164; E-mail: tseeker@earthscape.com
Client/Server Architect

Keyword Summary

Systems Engineer. Client Server System Architect. Systems Analysis. Systems Integration. Network Administration. Database Administration. Systems Administration. Software Engineering. Troubleshooting Computing Systems. C++. Visual Basic. SQL. UNIX Shell Script. Windows 1998. MS DOS. Windows NT. TCP/IP. OSI. Microsoft LAN Manager. Novell Netware. Project Management. Trade Studies. Consulting. BETA Tester. Technical Presentations. Sales Presentations. Instructor. BS Degree. Mathematics and Computer Science. UCLA. M.S. Degree. Computer Engineering.

Objective

Systems Engineer; Client/Server Systems Architect

Qualifications Summary

Nine years of experience in designing, installing, and troubleshooting computing systems; a proven track record in identifying problems and developing innovative solutions.

Technical Skills

Programming: C, C++, Visual BASIC, FORTRAN, Pascal, SQL, OSF/Motif, UNIX Shell Script (sh, ksh, csh), BASIC, Clipper, Algol 68, and 80X86 Assembler.

Operating Systems: UNIX (bsd & SVr3/r4), MS Windows, MS DOS, MS Windows NT, Solaris, HP-UX, Ultrix, AIX, VAX/VMS, and Macintosh System 7.

Networking: TCP/IP, OSI, Microsoft LAN Manager, Novell Netware, DDN, Internet, Ethernet, Token Ring, SNA, X.25, LAN-WAN interconnection.

Applications: Microsoft Office, Microsoft Access, Microsoft Visual C++, Microsoft Project, Microsoft Publisher, Lotus 123, Lotus Freelance, System Architect, among others.

Education

BS, Mathematics and Computer Science, University of California, Los Angeles, 1990.

Certification and Training

- Microsoft Certified Systems Engineer (MCSE #132546), August, 1997
- Microsoft Certified Product Specialist, TCP/IP Networking, June, 1997
- Transmission Control Protocol/Internet Protocol (TCP/IP), Technology Systems Institute, 1996.
- Database Administration, Performance Tuning, and Benchmarking with Oracle7, Oracle Corporation, 1995.
- Computer Systems Technology Program, Air Force Institute of Technology (AFIT), Graduate Courses in Software Engineering and Computer Communications (24 quarter units completed), 1992.

Professional Experience

Systems Engineer, Science Applications International Corporation (SAIC), McLean, VA, 1996–Present.

- Selected as the Systems Engineering Lead on a Federal agency terabyte database modernization project. This project centered on migrating from mainframe to client/server technology.
- Designed and managed the development of an enterprise-level client/server automated auditing application for the cost management division of a major long-distance telephone service provider. Migrated from mainframe computers, db2, and FOCUS to workgroup oriented, client/server architecture involving Windows for Workgroups, Windows NT Server, Microsoft SQL Server, Oracle7, and UNIX.
- Conducted extensive trade studies of a large number of vendors that offered leading-edge technologies; these studies identified proven (low-risk) implementations of symmetric multiprocessing computers (SMP) and Relational Database Management Systems (RDBMS) that met stringent performance and availability criteria.

Networks Administrator, Defense Information Systems Agency (DISA), Washington, D.C., 1990–1993

- Implemented and managed the Defense Message System (DMS) Central Test Facility; integrated over $117,000 in hardware and software.
- Proposed and obtained approval of a $1.6 million budget to develop the DMS Beta Testbed Network.
- Conducted a feasibility study on a development project that resulted in a $172,000 cost savings on planned equipment acquisitions.
- Recipient, Department of Defense Meritorious Service Medal.

Automated Data Processor, US Army Infantry, Germany, 1987–1990

- Designed a maintenance-reporting program that converted the laborious task of producing weekly status reports from a 4-day to a 2-hour process.
- Developed a departmental computer literacy training program, teaching classes on microcomputer operating systems, office automation software, and introductory programming.
- Taught a "Structured Programming and Problem Solving" course for the Community Education Center after work hours.

Chapter 6

Resumes as Electronic Messages

E-mail is the most widely used form of communication on the Internet, and the most direct method that you are likely to use when submitting your resume across the Internet. You can transport your resume to your intended audience within an e-mail message or as an attachment. In many cases, the attachment is a file that was created in a word processing program and saved in its native file format. Internet e-mail messages contain only standard ASCII characters—but have the ability to include binary file data in its "envelope."

Attachments can be both binary or ASCII files. They are encoded through two standards—the Simple Mail Transport Protocol (SMTP), and Multiple Internet Mail Extensions (MIME). MIME is a more recent development and is not totally implemented by all Internet users, which may cause compatibility problems. This problem is getting better, but when you're sending a document as important as a resume, you don't want to end up frustrating your potential hiring manager. Sometimes, plain text is just best.

Many employers and recruiters today request that you submit your resume via e-mail. That's because for many, e-mail is an ideal form of communication on the Internet because it is intimate and convenient. It is intimate because you can communicate with individuals privately, and both the sender and recipient have time to think about their replies. You can combine the clarity of text written on paper with the immediacy of a phone call, and send it at anytime you wish.

There are problems with attachments. Recruiters receive many resumes that cannot be translated into ASCII text only, leaving them to ask the sender to e-mail his or her resume back in a different format. Along with the potential problems, the challenge lies in knowing what software the person at the receiving end of your e-mail message is using.

E-mail basics

Depending on the capabilities of the e-mail program, users can also forward mail, include copies, attach files, edit messages, and reply back to the sender. Most ISPs offer some form of Internet e-mail.

E-mail is sent and received on either host-based e-mail systems, or LAN (Local Area Network)-based systems. Host-based systems are older e-mail systems, usually on mainframe or UNIX computers. These are text-based systems with little or no support for attachments. LAN-based systems use file sharing to handle e-mail delivery. These LAN-based systems support e-mail client software like Microsoft Outlook or Eudora Mailer. Because they are based on PCs, the LAN-based systems tend to be graphically oriented and provide richer attachment support. When you submit your resume via e-mail, its file is stored on the recipient's PC and viewed with his or her e-mail reader.

There are two kinds of ISP e-mail accounts that use a host-based system: POP3 e-mail and Web-based e-mail.

POP3

POP3, or Post Office Protocol version 3, is a standard set of rules that allows your e-mail client (software on your PC, such as Eudora or Microsoft Outlook) to access an electronic mailbox (an account set up by your ISP).

With POP3, incoming messages are stored on a server at your ISP. These messages remain there until you connect to the server using a POP3 client and download the messages onto your local computer (which is normally done automatically when you connect). Since these mail files are on your computer, you can work offline. Once you have downloaded your messages, you can disconnect from the Internet and then read and reply to your e-mail at your leisure. You can then reconnect to the Internet when it's time to send your replies.

Web-based e-mail

Web-based e-mail services allow you to retrieve your e-mail from a specified site via your Web browser. This means that you can access your e-mail from any computer that has Internet access and a Web browser.

Web-based e-mail is ideal for job-seekers who want to keep their online job search activities private, without having to use their e-mail address at work. There is a rising trend in the use of free Web-based e-mail services by people at work in order to hide their personal correspondence from corporate Internet-usage monitoring systems. You still have to log into the site you signed up with in order to gain access to your e-mail. But a Web-based e-mail account is an ideal job-search tool if your only other e-mail account is at work. Providing such an e-mail address is convenient for contacting you, without the potential embarrassment of a recruiter contacting you at work. You can easily log in and collect your e-mail from any Web browser. And, with the exception of some services like Juno (http://www.juno.com), there are no programs to configure in order to access e-mail. This is especially advantageous if you do not own a computer, but have access to a computer equipped with Internet access.

The limitation to Web-based e-mail is that in order to offer these services for free, you usually have to agree to placement of rotating advertising banners as you read your e-mail, which can slow down access to your messages and distract you as you are reading your messages. You will usually be shown banner advertisements while your e-mail is being retrieved.

There are many places online to find free e-mail. Some of the most popular are Microsoft's Hotmail (http://www.hotmail.com), Juno (http://www.juno.com), and Rocketmail (http://www.rocketmail.com). Some of the major search engines also offer free e-mail accounts, such as Yahoo's Yahoo Mail (http://www.yahoo.com) and Excite's Excite Mail (http://www.excite.com).

What your e-mail address can say about you

Whether you sign up for a POP3 e-mail account or a Web-based e-mail account, or both, when you set up an e-mail account for the purpose of conducting your online job search, you should consider what you choose as your e-mail address.

A typical e-mail address looks like this:
Tseeker@earthscape.com

where:

- "Tseeker" is the user account (or login) name.
- "@" separates the user name from the next part, the domain name.
- "earthscape.com" is the domain name.

When you select a user name, think about how easy it will be for your recipients to remember it. For example, an e-mail address like TWebs39214@aol.com is not only difficult to remember, it is also difficult to retype.

Also, think about the kind of impression you want to give with your e-mail address. For example, what if you are participating on a discussion forum where the topic of discussion is about disgruntled employees and their respective employers? Let's say your e-mail address shows up as tseeker@xerox.com as the sender of a message you post to the group. Not only can you inadvertently leave the impression that you are "bad-mouthing" your employer, you are also indicating that you are participating in activities that should be better handled after hours.

Formatting your resume for e-mail

Now that you have established your personal e-mail account, the next thing to consider is how you should format your resume for e-mail so that you can send successfully, without having to know what software the recipient is using.

Because e-mail is plain text and is universally recognized across different computer systems and networks, it makes sense that text-only resumes are best to consider when you don't know what software is being used at the other end.

Transferring files in plain text is important for another reason: In the recent past, employers would print resumes received via e-mail and then scan them into a database for electronic distribution. But employers are adapting newer technology that bypasses the scanning process altogether. Systems are being employed that place your e-mail resume directly into tracking databases. These databases store text data, making plain text resumes important.

For example, Microsoft uses Restrac (http://www.restrac.com) as its primary candidate database. Microsoft no longer scans resumes. It now saves the attachments and/or converts them into text files that are retrieved from Restrac. Microsoft no longer accepts fax copies of resumes to scan, because the data is often unusable with faxes.

Cargill, Inc. (http://www.cargill.com), an international marketer, processor, and distributor of agricultural, food, financial, and industrial products, has developed an efficient process for receiving resumes via e-mail. The company encourages applicants to send their resumes via e-mail because it saves them time in scanning information into their system. With e-mail, resumes are automatically downloaded into the database.

They advise that resumes sent via e-mail be in a specific format: The resume should be in the body of the e-mail message, and not as an attachment. The name, address, and e-mail address should be listed at the top left of the resume, followed by the resume text. The ideal length is one page, without any special formatting features such as bolding, underlining, italics, bullets, horizontal lines, or graphics.

Unfortunately, even though employers and recruiters ask for ASCII-text-only resumes, many people don't know how to ensure that the resume they send to them is in ASCII format.

ASCII plain text, step by step

So how do you transmit a copy of that gorgeous-looking resume you already have on file in your word processor? Following is an exercise that illustrates how you can convert an existing resume to text-only format. You can use Notepad, a text editor that comes with Windows 3.1 and Windows 95. Macintosh users tell me that Simple Text bundled with the operating system will accomplish the same. When you have completed this step-by-step exercise, compare your results to the ASCII resume that follows.

1. In your word processor document, set your margins so that you have 6.5 inches of text displayed.
2. Compose a resume from scratch or open an existing resume in your word processor. For this exercise, Microsoft Word 6.0 or higher was used.
3. Select all of the text, and then select a font that is nonproportional 12 pitch, such as Courier 12. This will give you 65 characters per line, which will accommodate most e-mail programs.

4. Save your resume as a "text only" file with "line breaks." If you have been instructed to use "hard" carriage returns at the end of paragraphs instead of lines, save as "text only" without the line breaks.

5. Open this new file in Notepad, or any other text editor that you can cut and paste text into.

6. Review your resume in the text editor. Notepad lets you view your resume as it will most likely be viewed by the recipient. Formatting characteristics such as proportional fonts will disappear because text editors display data in one fixed font, and it will indicate what part of your text contains unsupported ASCII characters such as bullets or underlining.

7. Replace all unsupported characters with their ASCII equivalent. For example, bullets created in Microsoft Word 6.0 or 7.0 appear as a question mark when opened in Notepad. They can be replaced with asterisks or hyphens. Any character found on your keyboard is an ASCII-equivalent character. If you see long lines of text in your editor, use Notepad's word wrap feature under the Edit menu. This feature inserts "hard" returns, allowing you to format the resume to meet specified margins. If you have been instructed to enter hard carriage returns at the end of paragraphs instead of lines, then do not use this word wrap feature.

8. Once you are satisfied with the way it looks in your text editor, copy and paste the text of the resume into the body of a test e-mail message.

9. Create a short cover letter. You can do this the same way you created your resume. Cut and paste this text above the resume in the e-mail message. Do not send the cover letter separately as an e-mail attachment.

10. Send a copy of this e-mail message to yourself and to a friend who is using a different e-mail program before transferring the text file to the recruiter to test compatibility.

What plain text looks like

Now compare your newly created text-only resume with the following example. It's not much to look at visually, but computers love it. You can use capital letters and spaces to enhance the "look and feel" of your resume.

Here is an example of what a plain text format resume might look like:

```
THOMAS B. SEEKER
4120 Bellow Drive, Baltimore, MD 21203
Voice: (410)555-8164; E-mail: tseeker@earthscape.com

OBJECTIVE: Systems Engineer;  Client/Server Systems Architect

QUALIFICATIONS SUMMARY
Nine years of experience in designing, installing, and troubleshooting
computing systems; a proven track record in identifying problems and de-
veloping innovative solutions.
```

TECHNICAL SKILLS
Programming: C, C++, Visual BASIC, FORTRAN, Pascal, SQL, OSF/Motif, UNIX Shell Script (sh, ksh, csh), BASIC, Clipper, Algol 68, and 80X86 Assembler.
Operating Systems: UNIX (bsd & SVr3/r4), MS Windows 1998, MS DOS, MS Windows NT, Solaris, HP-UX, Ultrix, AIX, VAX/VMS, and Mac OS 8.5.
Networking: TCP/IP, OSI, Microsoft LAN Manager, Novell Netware, DDN, Internet, Ethernet, Token Ring, SNA, X.25, LAN-WAN interconnection.

Applications: Microsoft Office, Microsoft Access, Microsoft Visual C++, Microsoft Project, Microsoft Publisher, Lotus 123, Lotus Free-lance, and others.

EDUCATION
BS, Mathematics and Computer Science, University of California, Los Angeles, 1990.

CERTIFICATIONS AND TRAINING
• Microsoft Certified Systems Engineer (MCSE #132546), August, 1997.
• Microsoft Certified Product Specialist, TCP/IP Networking, June, 1997.
• Transmission Control Protocol/Internet Protocol (TCP/IP), Technology Systems Institute, 1996.
• Database Administration, Performance Tuning, and Benchmarking with Oracle7, Oracle Corporation, 1995.
• Computer Systems Technology Program, Air Force Institute of Technology (AFIT), Graduate Courses in Software Engineering and Computer Communications (24 quarter units completed), 1992.

PROFESSIONAL EXPERIENCE
Systems Engineer
Science Applications International Corporation (SAIC), McLean, VA, 1996-Present
• Selected as the Systems Engineering Lead on a Federal agency terabyte database modernization project. This project centered on migrating from mainframe to client/server technology.
• Designed and managed the development of an enterprise-level client/server automated auditing application for the cost management division of a major long-distance telephone service provider. Migrated from mainframe computers, db2, and FOCUS to workgroup oriented, client/server architecture involving Windows for Workgroups, Windows NT Server, Microsoft SQL Server, Oracle7, and UNIX.
• Conducted extensive trade studies of a large number of vendors that offered leading-edge technologies; these studies identified proven (low-risk) implementations of symmetric multiprocessing computers (SMP) and Relational Database Management Systems (RDBMS) that met stringent performance and availability criteria.

Networks Administrator
Defense Information Systems Agency (DISA), Washington, D.C., 1990-1993
• Implemented and managed the Defense Message System (DMS) Central Test Facility; integrated over $117,000 in hardware and software.
• Proposed and obtained approval of a $1.6 million budget to develop the DMS Beta Testbed Network.
• Conducted a feasibility study on a development project that resulted in a $172,000 cost savings on planned equipment acquisitions.
• Recipient, Department of Defense Meritorious Service Medal.

```
Automated Data Processor
US Army Infantry, Germany, 1987-1990
• Designed a maintenance reporting program that converted the labori-
ous task of producing weekly status reports from a 4-day to a 2-hour
process.
• Developed a departmental computer literacy training program, teaching
classes on microcomputer operating systems, office automation software,
and introductory programming.
• Taught a "Structured Programming and Problem Solving" course for the
Community Education Center after work hours.
```

Sending your resume as an e-mail attachment

Before you decide to send your resume as an attachment, consider that many employers and resume listing services are requesting that you do not send attachments when responding to a job ad via e-mail.

An attachment is a separate but internal part of an e-mail message. When you send a message to somebody else as a convenience, you "attach" a file to ride along with your message.

Some e-mail programs don't support attachments at all. Some people receiving attachments will get "gobbledygook" and others don't, because they are unsupported by their client software. As a result, people will see strange characters at the end of the supported text at the bottom of their messages.

There are other operational reasons why attachments may not be popular with a particular e-mail recipient. For one, attachments can take up a lot of disk space, depending on what type of files they are and how many you receive at one time.

Depending on the e-mail program that you use, attachments are typically stored locally (on your hard drive) in a temporary directory. Some e-mail programs store attachments in a mail file until they are accessed. The application used to view or open the attachment, such as a word processor, expects to find those files on the hard drive.

The convenience of sending files in addition to text with your messages is inconvenienced by the possibilities of sending viruses. The very term "virus" implies a perceived threat to someone's computer system. This alone is enough to make any user wary of receiving attached files, especially if your potential employer did not ask for attachments.

If you do want to send your non-ASCII resume as an attachment, make sure that you scan it for viruses. Anti-virus software, such as those products listed in Appendix E has become a popular addition to what people install on their computers.

Sending cover letters as part of an e-mail message

On the Net, tailoring the electronic format of your resume is just as important as tailoring the content of a cover letter for the specific job you are applying for. In most cases, job candidates should also submit a cover letter with their resume in the body of the e-mail message, but not as an attachment.

If you know that your recipient uses attachments, place your cover letter in the body of your e-mail message, and send your resume as the attachment. This way you only include one attachment in the e-mail message itself.

As the Internet gains popularity, and resumes are reduced to ASCII characters and keywords, making your resume stand out becomes a greater challenge. Cover letters can play a valuable role as a selling tool. Use cover letters to supplement, not repeat the kind of information that should already be in your resume. When a candidate uses a cover letter for this latter purpose, it indicates to recruiters and hiring managers that the individual's resume has not been updated. Also, include the URL of your Web resume only if it is going to support, not replace, the ASCII version of your resume. A single URL specifies a page's location on the Internet. If you can spend the time to create a Web resume, you can also spend the time to create a text-only resume that can be pasted into the body of your e-mail message.

Don't send a cover letter via e-mail with just the URL to your Web resume. This is perceived as laziness, and conveys your lack of effort. Instead, preface your resume with a targeted cover letter that is short, adds something fresh, and can be read within the first screen.

Other things to avoid in your cover letter are smaller in importance, but crucial nonetheless. For example, avoid using all capital lettering in your letter. On the Internet, this comes off as shouting. Also, avoid using emoticons (smiley faces etc.). Emoticons are symbols used to convey body language taken for granted during face-to-face chatting. Not only do these come off as too casual, but you are assuming that everyone knows what they mean.

Creating your e-mail signature

If you want to create a link to your Web resume, a more tactful approach is to include it as part of your e-mail signature.

An e-mail signature can serve multiple purposes. You can include information similar to that found on a business card, as well as something that gives insight to your personality, such as a quote that best represents your outlook on life.

An e-mail signature is very much like a signature block found at the end of business correspondence. For e-mail purposes, it is text that is automatically appended to all of your outgoing messages.

Many e-mail programs can automatically append the contents of a signature file to the very end of each message you send. A signature file contains only ASCII text. You can include your name, phone number, e-mail address, and home page URL in your signature.

Once you type in what you want in your signature, your e-mail program will add it to the bottom of all of your outgoing messages. Some e-mail programs will let you create several signatures, which you can invoke as needed. In Microsoft Outlook, for example, you can access the **AutoSignature** feature from the **Tools** Menu.

To create your signature,

1. Go to **Tools** | **Options** | **Edit**.
   You should see your signature information immediately in the "user" category.
2. Edit your signature and click **Ok** when finished.

A general rule is to avoid making your signature more than four to five lines long, not to exceed 60 to 65 characters per line.

If you have a Web resume, make sure you include the entire URL. Typing out the full URL (with `http://`) will cause newer versions of e-mail programs to display the text as an actual hyperlink. It also serves as a convenience for those using older Web browsers to copy and paste your URL right into their browser.

E-mail signatures also come in handy when you are participating in e-mail-based newsgroups and LISTSERVs for career networking. If someone has an interest in what you are saying, he or she has a way of contacting you.

Also, if you have a Web resume, you should include its URL in your e-mail signature. Not only does this allow interested people to link to it, but the URL to your Web resume can be picked up by the major search engines that index newsgroups for this kind of information.

Here's what an e-mail signature looks like:

```
* * * * * * * * * * * * * * * * * * * * * * * * * * * * * * * * * * * * * * * * * * * * * * * * * * * * * *

Thomas B. Seeker
Client/Server Architect
E-mail: tseeker@earthscape.com
Web: http://www.earthscape.com/~tseeker/resume.html
Voice: (410) 555-8164

* * * * * * * * * * * * * * * * * * * * * * * * * * * * * * * * * * * * * * * * * * * * * * * * * * * * * *
```

Plain and simple is better

Whether you send a resume as the body of an e-mail message or as an e-mail attachment really depends on who you are sending your resume to.

If possible, ask the employer which is preferable. But when in doubt, send it within the e-mail message. It's content, not beauty that will get you noticed.

Just as the objective statement of your resume minimizes the guesswork of determining what kind of job you are interested in, creating a plain text version of your resume that accommodates most computer systems will maximize the likelihood that it will be read.

Here are some things to remember about your e-resume:

1. Start your resume with a flush left margin of 0, keeping your right margins at 6.5" in order to accommodate most word processors and computer screens.

2. When sending your resume in the e-mail message, remove all formatting codes from the text file. Avoid the use of bullets, underlining, boldface, or italics.

3. If your e-mail supports attachments, send it as a "text only" file.

4. The standard font of an ASCII file is usually a Courier-based font, and is always fixed (nonproportional).

5. If the file is to be transferred as unformatted text and was created in a word processor, use its **Save As** feature to save it as an ASCII text file.

Newsgroups and binary files

Because newsgroups use the same technology as e-mail, everything said about using binary files (word-processing files, sounds, video, and so on) holds true for newsgroups. E-mail, newsgroups, and mailing lists all rely on Internet e-mail technology to transmit and receive simple messages and computer files. Both text and binary files can be transferred, but because e-mail can only transfer text, binary files must be encoded into text files using protocols such as MIME and SMTP. Most new e-mail programs use MIME for encoding, but some older e-mail programs may not be able to decode MIME. Keep this in mind when sending out e-resumes on a newsgroup. A resume is useless if it cannot be read by potential employers.

Chapter 7

Resumes as Part of Electronic Forms

Electronic forms, also known as e-forms, are much like those employment application forms that you are asked to complete when you arrive at a job interview. E-forms require the sender to manually input text into specified fields on a Web page, and then click on a button to submit the information. At that time, the data entered into these specified fields is stored in a database. E-forms process information as ASCII text only.

The limitation of electronic forms, depending on how they are implemented, is that many Web browsers may not support them. People using those browsers may not be able to use those forms. However, Netscape Communicator and Internet Explorer, the two most popular Web browsers, do support e-forms.

For the job-seeker, the benefit of e-forms over e-mail is that you know exactly what to include on your resume before posting it. You no longer have to debate over whether to include a keyword summary or an objective statement, or whether you should use bullets. You can also research and organize the information to include in your resume ahead of time before you complete the form. The more detailed the form, the more information you have about what to include.

On the other hand, this level of detail can be its downfall: If the e-forms are too complicated to fill out, people won't use them. It can get incredibly frustrating as you encounter instructions such as:

Many browsers can only display 60-70 characters of text wide, so be sure to look at the resume section once you have submitted this form to see what the final result looks like.

If you encounter a problem with pasting your resume into the form, try using the keyboard macro command for "paste." If you're on a PC, the command is "control + V"—so hold down the control key while you press V. If you're on a Mac the procedure is "command + V" (or apple + V).

At present, our system does not accept free form resumes or resumes created elsewhere. The resume has ten (10) different sections that should be completed as applicable.

Once the resume is accepted by our server, it will assign a NUMBER to it. Write this number down. (Hint: you can print the page and save it.) You will need this number to access it again for updating or to respond to a job.

Wow! That's a lot of work! Not only does this become a frustrating process that requires that you know a lot about browsers, copying and pasting text, and even understanding what text is, there are other questions raised, as well. Rather than go through lists of Web sites and review them individually here, let's address three popular concerns among job-seekers regarding these e-forms, and provide examples of job boards to illustrate these points.

How do I cut and paste my resume into an e-form?

In some e-forms, there are individual, customized data fields that require you to enter data in small "pieces." In others, there are large fields to cut and paste whole resume parts into. A method that is becoming more and more popular is to copy and paste your entire resume into a data field.

Begin by manually filling out the required information fields. In some instances, the form is very detailed—you list your job objective, skills, and work history into pre-defined data fields. Also, if you have a great deal of experience, you are not restricted by the traditional one- to two-page resume. You want to include as many important keywords as you can so that people can find you when searching the database. When you are contacted, you can personally send a shorter, paper version of your resume.

CareerWeb (http://www.careerweb.com), for example, used to require that you complete a highly detailed form had fields for information as detailed as providing "up to five specific examples and descriptions of your skills" for each "primary field of expertise." Now you just have to complete basic information such as name, address, years of experience, and salary range. Then you are prompted to cut and paste a cover letter and your resume into two separate data fields.

HeadHunter.net has a similar data field into which you cut and paste your entire resume. There is no separate data field for a cover letter.

To copy and paste, select the text from your resume that you want to copy. Choose **Edit | Copy**, go to the form field where you want to paste your text, then choose **Edit | Paste**.

At other career sites, such as The Monster Board (http://www.monster.com), you may also be asked to select a category or categories that best match your area of interest from among a list of categories. If you're not sure which categories to choose, select all of the categories in the applicable industry. To make multiple selections, hold down the control key (PC) or command key (Mac) while clicking on the desired location by grouping job titles into subgroups or categories. Similar positions are grouped together with a pointer; for example, "Engineering" groups together all engineering jobs.

Many times you are also required to register by selecting a username and password either before or after you fill out the form. In other instances, you register, and a password will be sent to you via e-mail.

A username is sometimes referred to as your nickname or screen name. It is the name that appears on your screen to greet you when you log in to your account. A password provides you access to your account. It should be easy for you to remember, but not for others to guess.

In the case of HeadHunter.net (`http://www.headhunter.net`), you may use an alternate screen name if you wish to conceal your identity (to keep your online resume a secret from your boss).

How will your e-form look when viewed?

Once you have completed and submitted your resume via the electronic form, many job boards let you view it, edit it, and then resubmit it once you have posted it. CareerWeb and HeadHunter.net both let you use these editing features.

When you submit your resume via an electronic form, its data is stored into a database and viewed by the database's software interface. The data format is either ASCII or HTML.

To create your resume in the ASCII text-only format, you can type it directly into the e-form. Alternatively, you can take your existing resume that you have created in a popular word processing program and save it as text only. Then you simply cut and paste it into the resume e-form. When cutting and pasting, be sure that the data you enter is ASCII text only. Refer to Chapter 6 for a review of these steps.

As you learned in Chapter 6, when you do this you will lose many of the formatting features that you included in your original resume. However, you can replace all unsupported characters with their ASCII equivalent. For example, bullets created in Microsoft Word 6.0 or 7.0 appear as a question mark when opened in Notepad. They can be replaced with asterisks or hyphens.

Some e-forms will instruct you to insert "hard" returns after each line you type into the form. You can do this automatically by using a text editor such as Notepad to wrap words. This feature inserts "hard" returns, allowing you to format the resume to meet specified margins.

About rich text format

One job board had this to say:

> *"You can adapt your existing resume easily by saving the resume using your word processing package as a 'text only' or a 'rich text' document."*

This might stump you at first, as I just stated that plain ASCII text-only is the best way to send your resume via e-mail or to post to an e-form. Rich text format (`.rtf`) is also ASCII text, but it includes formatting instructions with the text, which to some software packages will arrive as garbage. Try opening any file that you saved in your word processor, and save it as "rich text format." Close it. Now try opening the file you saved as rich text format in your text editor, and you'll see the formatting instructions included in the text.

By focusing on text-only, you can increase your chances of your resume looking the way you sent it for the majority of instances that you submit your resume.

To save an .rtf word-processed file, use the **Save As** command of the word processor. This file can then be imported into the same or another word processor while preserving the original format. Be aware that word processors may have slightly different features regarding their implementation of .rtf formats. The following are some general guidelines currently in use for preparing your resume in .rtf format.

- Find out what word processor the recipient uses, and save your resume file in that word processor's native format.
- If you know the recipient has a word processor, but don't know which one, save the file in .rtf format.
- Insert the file into your e-mail message as an attachment. If you do not know how to do this, do one of three things:

  1. Check your application's user documentation.
  2. Ask your systems administrator.
  3. Contact your service provider.

What are the chances of getting a response?

There are no guarantees that employers will come knocking on your virtual door. At the same time, careful planning, strategic posting, and routine monitoring are the best guarantees against having your resume float uselessly all over the Internet.

Whether you are actively looking for a job or just want to know the current job trends in your field, job boards are proving to be a valuable resource in your online job search. By taking advantage of job boards, you are armed with more information regarding the company and the kinds of skills they are looking for.

Each posting service offers different ways of accessing resume databases. Some allow employers and job candidates direct access to the database. Others do not allow employers to casually browse through the resumes they have on file. Instead, employers tell the job-search service what kind of job they want to fill, along with the qualifications they are expecting from the prospective employee. After the employer "orders" his candidates, a database service employee searches their records.

Does the database post the kinds of jobs that interest you?

Follow up your selection with criteria such as overall reputation and ability to update and delete your resume at will. Many niche sites are becoming much more popular. For example, there are specialized job boards that cater to the automotive, fashion, and hospitality industries. See Appendix A for a comprehensive listing of Web sites and other metaindustry-job boards that have been around for quite awhile.

Would your ideal employer search the system you're posting on?

Research the job boards for corporate sponsorships. Many job boards provide links to or list the kinds of companies that use their services. For example, The CareerBuilder Network (http://www.careerbuilder.com) informs you of what companies are posting job announcements on their job board. Job boards like The Monster Board (http://www.monster.com) and CareerMosaic (http://www.careermosaic.com) help focus your search by displaying companies hiring in a requested industry or geographic location.

Try to take advantage of those job boards that let you apply directly to the employer. This is what makes The Monster Board an ideal resource. You can opt to fill out its electronic form, but you also have the option of researching the job listings, and follow the links to an employer's Web site. This lets you apply to the company directly, giving you some sense of control over who is getting your resume.

How long does a resume stay on the system?

Some job boards keep your resume in their database indefinitely, or until you request that it be deleted from their database.

On CareerWeb, your resume expires after 90 days. On the 80th day, CareerWeb will send you an e-mail reminder so that you can renew your resume posting for another 90-day period if you choose. Be sure to find out how long your resume will stay active on any database that you post to.

What feedback do you get when someone views your resume?

Many job boards now offer sophisticated tools that let job-seekers monitor the effectiveness of their posted resume. CareerSite (http://www.careersite.com), for example, provides job-seekers with a personal message center where they can find employers who want to contact them. This gives job-seekers opportunity to determine if certain jobs are of interest to them, and whether to disclose their identity. JobOptions (http://www.joboptions.com) goes one step further by providing job-seekers a feature that lets them see how many times their resume has been viewed.

Job search agents

Job search agents are computer programs that automatically scan and return information from a site's database, based on search data that a job-seeker fills out in an online form. Some of the most familiar kinds of agents are those used in search engines. All you do is complete an online form, and these agents will find jobs that match your profile. Results are sent to you on a regular basis via e-mail.

Agent technology gives job-seekers the ability to automatically search for and deliver jobs directly to their desktop—a great feature for busy job-seekers currently employed who might want to test the waters but don't have the time to invest in an extensive job search. Agent technology helps to ensure that job boards don't deliver jobs that are not relevant. Also, the preferences selected when completing an e-form assist career-changing job-seekers in venturing into other occupations.

Job-search agent technology provides application-based solutions for both employers and job-seekers based on the latest developments in database, messaging, and agent technology. When the candidate completes a personal profile by completing the online form, or e-form, he or she enters information that identifies desired jobs, location, skills, and qualifications for those jobs.

When an employer runs a search of the candidate database, the candidate's profile is presented to the employer. If the employer is interested in the candidate, the employer interactively "invites" the candidate to respond to their job opportunity via e-mail. Employers will only receive responses from interested job-seekers.

Job-seekers only respond to jobs they are interested in. By getting jobs that match their profile sent to them via e-mail, they don't have to waste time scrolling through screen after screen to find appropriate jobs. Nor do they want to recreate their resume or send a generic-looking resume that might be scanned. Scanning resumes introduces another factor that may eliminate job-seekers. If their resume is not translated correctly by the computer when it is scanned, the job-seeker may be eliminated from the company's database.

However, there are some positive factors: As Sandra Grabczynski, director of employer development at CareerSite points out, the primary step in any recruitment process is finding qualified candidates. Rather than worrying about job-seekers sorting through jobs, and employers having to screen thousands of potential applications, the job-seeker can focus on job opportunities based on a personal profile, and an employer can focus on qualified candidates that have expressed interest in the job. Many job boards are now incorporating job-search agents into their job-searching services.

Despite the usefulness of job search agents, the process of posting your resume on the Internet does not necessarily guarantee your confidentiality. The best guarantee of your privacy is to not give out your personal information in the first place. Also, when posting to job boards, it's a good idea to consider using job-search services that e-mail job notices to you, rather than posting your entire resume into a resume database. Not only does this let you filter the jobs you are really interested in, it also minimizes the possibility that your employer will come across your resume. In some cases you don't have to submit any personal information unless you want to respond directly to a job notice that is sent to you. This lets you assert even more control over the distribution of your resume, and still provide a way for recruiters to contact you.

Developers.net (`http://www.developers.net`) is a good example of this distribution method. Developers.net (see Figure 1) is a job board that specializes in the high-technology industry.

Figure 1. Developers.net at `http://www.developers.net`

Developers.net recognizes that job-seekers will not spend time on an online service providing a lot of personal information about themselves. The only requirement at Developers.net is to submit your e-mail address, and select two other pieces of information: your platform expertise for software development, and what location you would like to work.

Jobs that correspond to the geographical area(s) you've chosen will be forwarded to your e-mail address. If you like what you see, you may reply with your resume. Developers.net presents your resume to the hiring company and that company will contact you personally. You can also browse job descriptions at your convenience.

Job agents provide good feedback. By posting your resume to several job boards that have agents and are focused on your area of interest, you can measure the results for yourself by the responses you receive.

Chapter 8

Resumes as Personal Web Pages

Web resumes are flexible low-cost alternatives to the usual distribution process of resumes. Furthermore, they showcase your talents to the widest possible audience and allow you to be in several places at once—24 hours a day. Just as you "work a room" when attending a networking event, by integrating basic Web page design with resume-development principles, you can reach a much broader audience working the Web.

Some may argue that recruiters and hiring staff don't have time to surf the net looking at resumes. With the current job market favoring the candidate, recruiters are increasingly using the Web to get a sense of who's in the job marketplace. Unemployment is at its lowest and there are more jobs to fill than there are candidates to place. Hence, recruiters can't ignore the Web. It is a gold mine containing thousands of resumes—without cost. For example, when searching on the Internet via the Yahoo! search engine, type the keywords "individual resumes," and you'll find thousands of Web resumes posted by individuals, listed by category.

Here's what one successful job-seeker said about her Web resume:

When I originally posted my resume, I did not anticipate that it would actually be productive from the perspective of finding a job. From everything I had heard, (a) no one would go looking for a high-level employee, especially in a non-computer-related area on the Net (I'm a partner at a big law firm); and (b) in the conservative world of law firms, just having a resume online might be seen as unconventional enough to actually turn away potential employers.

To her surprise this was not the case. She continues:

...What has happened has been that the online resume has been far and away my most successful job-hunting technique—more effective than search firms that use conventional methods to find jobs in my field.

She then listed several of her experiences. Here are a few:

...An amazing number of people really do surf the Net looking for potential new hires—often as an initial step before starting a more intensive search. This has been beneficial in terms of introducing me to potential employers I might

never have come into contact with otherwise—and perhaps of having them like me enough to hire me instead of going through a search for other candidates.

...Those people who contact me through the Net have been more compatible with me personally than potential employers I have contacted through other mechanisms. Those people who would read a resume on the Net, and call the person in for an interview, tend to be creative and approachable—the very people I would like to work with.

...Developing my Web resume gave me some new skills that I could demonstrate in job interviews. In one instance, I did a critique of a potential employer's corporate Web site, which I had researched for more information on them prior to the interview. Firms are constantly looking for new ways to bring in clients, of which a Web site is one way. Potential partners who can intelligently discuss ways of promoting their firm over the Internet get extra points.

...The Web resume is a quick way of getting to potential employers, without having it arrive as a washed-out fax copy. My regular online resume is linked to a plain text version. Someone who is interested in me and who wants to send my resume around to his or her partners can print out the text version—even on traditional plain bond paper—and have it look like a regular printed resume.

Web resumes revealed

Simply stated, a Web resume is a Web document containing hyperlinked, "clickable" text and images created in HTML. Whatever you can do on paper, you can do on the Web with ease and creativity. Web resumes demonstrate accomplishments and expertise with a personal style that is lost in traditional paper resumes. With a Web resume, you can communicate as much information about yourself as needed to achieve your career goals.

On the Web, costs do not increase as the amount of information you communicate increases. With paper resumes, size is a constraining factor, as they must be kept to one or two pages for the sake of the review process. Paper resumes beyond two pages reflect badly on the applicant, because they are too wordy. Web resumes are different, since the job-seeker can put on a huge multimedia presentation for an employer and have him or her begging for more. Skilled users can make Web pages that bring text, graphics, audio, and video together to showcase their skills!

For example:

- A costume designer uses her Web resume to archive photos of her costume designs for several drama productions at theaters across the nation.
- A media and broadcast professional provides audio clips of his work in producing jingles, radio spots, and promos using digital-editing equipment.
- A technical writer provides links to actual work samples of online help documentation that she wrote.

- A graphic artist includes a short multimedia slideshow illustrating work done for a national magazine.
- A freelance Web designer provides current links to his works in progress as well as links to completed projects.
- A college graduate demonstrates his abilities to provide online technical support by incorporating a detailed form in his Web resume that invites recruiters to comment or ask questions on the spot.

Web resumes provide a perfect opportunity to develop online portfolios of accomplishments, incorporating items considered taboo in traditional paper resumes—photographs, written testimonials, and personal paragraphs. The Web now touches all areas of business and improves the way business is done by reducing cost and increasing revenue. Portfolio-style Web resumes aren't just for artists, writers, and designers. The trend in the growing demand for technically skilled workers with both technical and nontechnical job descriptions requires a greater familiarity with computers. Recruiters are discovering that a good place to find employees comfortable with computers is through the Internet.

Web resumes can be as large as you want, and visitors to Web resumes can choose to concentrate on what interests *them*. Links are important navigational aids that allow visitors to quickly and easily locate information. By clicking text or images, a series of actions is initiated. The two most common actions are to link to another part of the same Web page or to link to another page on the Web.

For example, you can establish links at the beginning of your resume to important categories within that resume. These might include hyperlinks to your specialized training and certifications. This allows the viewer the most direct way to the information they need to know.

However, links must be used with judgment. Keep your audience focused on your objective—don't let them "get lost" in external links and forget to return to your page. Use links to support, not distract, the viewer. Adding a link to an employer's Web site, such as IBM, will leave viewers wandering through IBM pages and, chances are, they will lose interest in returning to your resume.

If a page in your Web resume scrolls down several screens, you can provide links that let viewers jump back to the top of the page, or jump back to a major section of the resume. Links also provide immediate contact with you via e-mail hyperlinks. Instructions for creating links are provided in Chapter 9.

The unique nature of the Web is that information can be updated daily or as frequently as you like. Changes to your Web resume can be posted the day you make them. After you have added, deleted, or updated the information in your Web resume, it takes only seconds to post your pages to the Web using the File Transfer Protocol (FTP)—a common file-transmission method that is discussed in greater detail in Chapter 9. Compare this to the time-consuming process traditionally associated with maintaining a current paper resume that could add days or weeks to getting it distributed in its updated form.

On average, we will hold 3.5 careers in our lifetime and work for 10 employers, keeping each job 3.5 years (Department of Labor statistics). Add to that the likelihood of multiple working arrangements in a contract, freelance, or temporary capacity. A perpetual resume, one that is constantly up-to-date, lets you stay in touch with the job market as you look for continuous employment opportunities.

Rather than mailing your resume to several different employers, you post your resume in one location on the Web, and recruiters actively look for it. This poses a two-pronged resume development challenge for the job-seeker—leading prospective employers to your Web site and managing the appearance of your Web resume.

Looking for documents on the Web

Using a Web browser, such as Microsoft Internet Explorer or Netscape Navigator, you can access documents on the Web that can contain text, graphics, and references to other pages of information. These programs allow you to click on a reference to see other related pages.

Think of the Web as a large city (see Figure 1 on page 88). In a city, buildings are linked together by a series of streets, avenues, and freeways. You can get from one building to any other building in a city by traveling on a series of streets.

In this example, the buildings represent Web servers that store data in the form of documents. A Web server is a computer that makes documents available to others on the Internet. By using an address called a URL (Uniform Resource Locator), you can access a specific Web page stored on one of those servers. If you have a document in mind, you tell the Web browser where you want to go by typing the URL.

The general syntax of a URL is as follows:

```
protocol://host.domain/directory and resource filename
```

- `protocol` is the type of resource protocol being used, followed by a semicolon and two forward slashes.
- `host` is the name of the information server followed by a period.
- `domain name` is the location where the information server resides, followed by a single forward slash.
- `directory and resource filename information` is the path and directory location and name of the file being accessed, separated by single forward slashes to indicate the pathname.

Sample URLs:
- `http://java.sun.com/faq2.html`
- `ftp://ftp.fedworld.gov/pub/jobs/jobs.htm`

EXAMPLE:

`http://www.city.net/countries/united_states/california/san_francisco /maps/index.html` links to a site that provides maps of San Francisco, where `http` is the URL transfer protocol, `www.city.net` is the site's domain name, and `/countries/united_states/california/san_francisco/maps/index.html` is the directory and resource filename.

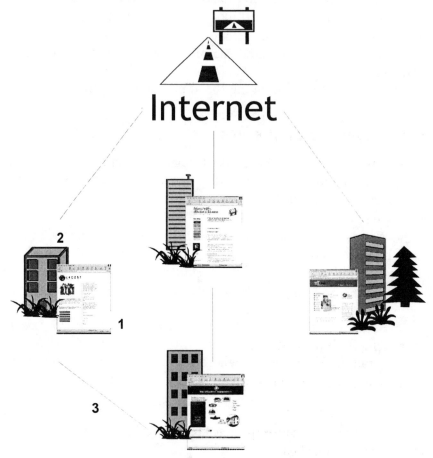

Figure 1. The World Wide Web is immensely popular because of its ease of use.

Managing how documents look on the Web

When you click a hyperlink in a Web page, it tells the Web browser to locate the computer on the Internet on which the requested document resides. If the document is available, the Web browser requests it, the Web server sends it to your computer, and the Web browser displays it on your computer screen.

The majority of Web pages are created in HTML, usually identified by the `.htm` or `.html` file extension. Because HTML is platform and browser independent, Windows, Macintosh, or UNIX users can use the same HTML code to publish Web pages using readily available HTML tools.

HTML was never originally designed for interaction and graphics. It was used as a structural tool to organize and transfer information over the Web, the structure indicated levels of main ideas, headers, sub-ideas, sub-headers, etc. It was at the University of Illinois that the first multimedia browser, Mosaic, was developed to support text and graphics. These inventors of Mosaic went on to start the Netscape Communications company.

Creating Web pages requires an understanding and familiarity with basic HTML common to all versions. By learning "raw" HTML, you can evaluate various authoring packages for use in your particular situation. Instructions for creating an HTML document are provided in Chapter 9.

An HTML document file contains all necessary information for the construction of a Web page. But it is the browser's job to put it together visually. HTML tags contain only generic labels for describing types of information. They don't allow for font or size specifications or any of the things resume writers are accustomed to choosing.

How HTML looks

A Web resume is an HTML document. An HTML document consists of text and tags. The text is the bulk of the page. The tags provide instructions to the browser on how to display the information found on that document. Converting text to HTML involves combining ASCII text with tags that contain formatting information. When a browser encounters each tag, it uses either its own built-in defaults or the user's chosen settings to display the formatted information. The basic HTML document structure is as follows:

```
<HTML>
<HEAD>
<TITLE> My Web Resume </TITLE>
<BODY>
...[page text]
</BODY>
</HEAD>
</HTML>
```

Tags can be typed in upper or lower case. Most tags come in pairs, where the first tag turns on a formatting command and the second tag turns it off (indicated by the "/" within the angled brackets). Such tags are commonly referred to as containers. Tags define the style to use when displaying information through a Web browser.

Because browsers receive Web pages as sets of instructions, how a Web page appears depends upon what browser you are using. Furthermore, Web pages don't look the same on 14-inch VGA monitors as on 17-inch SVGA monitors or at different screen resolutions. Colors also shift, depending upon the graphics card the viewer uses and the color display settings. It is this unpredictable nature of designing personal Web sites that makes Web resumes fundamentally different from paper resumes. How individuals configure their browsers, typography, size, and color can all affect how your page is displayed. The design of your Web resume should accommodate the most configurations.

As you build more sophisticated Web resumes, there comes a point where some page elements simply refuse to work the way you want, regardless of the page creation tools used. For that reason, a basic understanding of HTML allows you to go into your Web page HTML code, find the problem, and tweak it until it performs the way you want it to perform. Most authoring tools create dependency by generating cryptic and poorly formatted HTML. Once you've created a page with an authoring tool, it can be difficult to adjust the page at the HTML level. Instructions for creating an HTML document from scratch are provided in Chapter 9.

How HTML looks through a Web browser

While Web browsers are used to retrieve pages on the Web, HTML defines how those pages are rendered in the browser once retrieved, as shown in Figure 2. The HTML tags "mark up" the text and graphics found in the pages to be displayed. For example, text enclosed in the italics tag pair as "<I> My Web Resume </I>" displays as *My Web Resume.*"

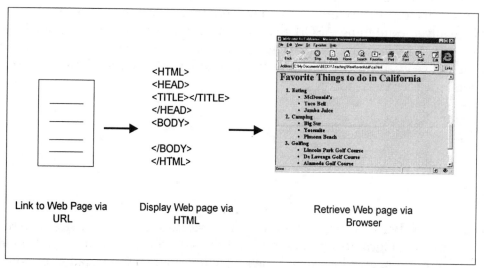

Figure 2. Browsers retrieve pages on the Web. HTML defines how those pages will look in the browser.

Page layout challenges

A Web page isn't limited by the traditional size of a traditional paper resume. Because it is a computer file, it can expand indefinitely. However, Web resumes represent the closest thing to traditional paper ones because you can create an exact replica with added flexibility. You can choose to link among multiple pages, scroll down pages that are longer than the traditional length, and divide a page into separate regions that contain different information.

There are two fundamental differences in the layout of your Web resume. For one, people don't like to scroll left and right on their computer screen. If recruiters are required to scroll across pages, they may be discouraged from studying your resume. To remedy this, try using tables. Tables are great for controlling left and right margins on your visitor's screen. Because a single table as long as your page can add to download time, try working around this by using multiple tables instead. Establish your margins based on a visitor using a 15- or 17-inch computer monitor.

In addition, many people find reading from a computer screen harder than reading from the printed page. Keep this in mind when designing your Web site. The first page of your Web resume should not be more than three screens long when viewed at 640x480 or 800x600 screen resolution.

You also have less control over how your audience views your page in contrast to a paper resume. With paper resumes, each one looks the same as the one before. With a Web resume, there are many variations in the hardware and software visitors use to view it. What may look one way to *you* will look differently to another viewer. As mentioned before, Web browsers can be configured to change the appearance of fonts other than what you selected for your pages. Therefore, the tools and techniques that you use in the design of your Web resume should accommodate the most people without knowing what hardware and software they will use.

Using frames in your Web page will allow you to have greater control over your site's appearance and function. Frames are rectangular subdivisions of the page that hold different pieces of information. You can place one or more frames on a page (referred to as the *frameset* for that page). Imagine your resume divided horizontally into two regions, each of which is a frame. The top frame is occupied by a row of links to sections throughout your resume. The contents of the frame on the bottom of the screen change, depending upon what link you clicked in the top frame. If you click a link labeled "Employment History" in the top frame, the section with the Employment History heading appears in the lower half of the screen. While frames can be useful, be wary of using them, as some browsers still do not support them.

Tables are another layout feature that help organize Web page information, similar to how tables organize information in a word processor file. However, when using tables or frames, you don't want to rely on them too heavily if you think your target audience might view your Web resume with a browser that doesn't support these layout features. Sometimes the simplest Web resume with just your name, contact information, skills, education, and qualifications is all that's needed to get your message across effectively. Your time would be better spent optimizing your HTML code for proper indexing by the major search than trying to use table and frame layout features to improve the "look" of your Web resume.

Graphics challenges

Graphics can make a Web page stand out above others in the minds of potential employers. However, graphics can cause Web pages to load slowly. Load time can be affected by the file size and color depth of the graphic being displayed, the number of people logged in to your Internet Service Provider, and/or the number of people concurrently accessing your Web page. For graphics to be used effectively, they must download as quickly as possible. Recruiters with a slow connection may lose interest in your resume if they must wait for a photograph to load. Instructions for inserting an image into a Web resume, as well as how to capture an existing image from the Web, are provided in Chapter 9.

Your modem is your key to the online world. It connects your computer to the telephone line, letting you communicate with other people with modem-equipped computers around the world. When thinking of modems, speed is a crucial commodity. The faster your modem, the less time it takes to transmit data. Modem speed is listed in bits per second (bps) or kilobits per second (kbps). The larger the number, the more bits of data a modem can transmit in a second. Slower speeds are usually listed in bits per second (for example, 9600 bps); faster speeds are listed in kilobits per second (for example, 28. 8 kbps).

Using a 28.8 kbps modem, a typical Web page without graphics (file size of approximately 10 KB) takes about three seconds to download to a browser. Standard desktop modem speeds currently range between 14.4, 28.8, 33.6, and 56 kbps. However, faster modem speed doesn't always mean faster access, upload, or download times. Modem speed doesn't take into account latency caused by the load, or the quality of connections between servers. Sometimes modems are held up by network outages or disconnections.

Also, while 56 kbps modems may download at 56 kbps, they can only upload files at 33.6 kbps. For example, if you include a 30 KB photograph of yourself in the resume, it could take an additional nine seconds to download your page. That's about 12 seconds per Web page. Now, take six Web resumes that are one page each multiplied by 12 seconds, and a recruiter is spending easily over a minute just in download time before beginning to read each resume. In an online world of subsecond response and dwindling attention spans, waiting 30 seconds or longer for anything could certainly lose your audience's attention.

Viewing other resumes on the Web

One of the best ways to gain an appreciation of the elements that go into developing a successful Web resume is to learn by observing the resumes of others on the Web. You can see the actual HTML code used to create each resume by viewing the source code of the file:

- **Microsoft Internet Explorer:** Choose **View | Source**.
- **Netscape Navigator:** Choose **View | Page Source**.

You can find thousands of resumes posted on the Web, as listed in the following sections. You can also find links to Web resumes posted by industry and individuals on the companion Web site, `http://www.eresumes.com/gallery_rezcat.html`.

Online resume and recruitment services

There are several no-cost resume and professional recruitment services that assist recruiters and job-seekers on the Web. Some of these services require that you first register, and then allow searching without cost:

A+ Online Resumes
http://www.ol-resume.com

View resumes listed alphabetically by professional discipline. A good source for liberal arts professionals.

Careerfile's Library of Resumes
http://www.careerfile.com

Free resume searches upon registration.

HeadHunter.net
http://www.headhunter.net/resfnd.htm

Full-featured free employment site without fees. Posting and searching for jobs and resumes is also free.

ORAsearch
http://www.orasearch.com

Search as a guest and view resumes of ORACLE professionals available for contract or permanent positions, worldwide.

Resume Innovations Search Engine
http://resume-innovations.com/search.html

View actual hypertext resumes using this search engine.

Resumes on the Web
http://www.resweb.com

Free site with a limited supply of resumes to view. It provides a good mix of technical and nontechnical categories for browsing.

ResumeWorld
http://www.resunet.com/cgi-bin/gate2?resunet|/rw

View hundreds of individual resumes. A little slow, but extensive and free.

CareerMagazine's Resume Bank
http://www.careermag.com/db/cmag_ressearch_form

Contains resumes of job-seekers submitted to *CareerMagazine* and downloaded daily from major Internet resume newsgroups.

CareerShop.com
http://www.careershop.com

Free resume searches upon registration. Another favorite place where recruiters post jobs for free.

Professional Association of Resume Writers

http://www.parw.com

Excellent resource for locating professional resume writers in your area, as well as for viewing samples of their work on the Web. Search the directory by state, city, or area code, then follow supporting links to those Web sites.

College and university Web sites

Many college and university departments host space on their servers where students can post resumes for a particular academic department. Alumni associations are also good sources of links to member home pages. Try these for starters:

Personal Pages Worldwide—College and University Collections

http://www.utexas.edu/world/personal/index.html

Extensive list of individual Web pages maintained at the University of Texas, Austin.

ScholarStuff—Colleges & Universities Worldwide Directory

http://www.scholarstuff.com/colleges/colleges.htm

Comprehensive directory of college and university Web sites around the world.

Cal Poly MBA Association

http://pozo.calpoly.edu:8000/mba/cgi-bin/list.cgi

View resumes of interns and graduates.

Howard University School of Engineering

http://www.cldc.howard.edu/HU/Schools/Engineering/resumes.html

View resumes of students in the Lewis K. Downing School of Engineering, and of nonengineering students in the Computer Learning and Design Center.

Kuala Lumpur Online—Universities & Colleges Worldwide

http://www.jaring.my/infokl/www/universities/unidir.htm

Comprehensive gateway resource for locating colleges or universities worldwide. Once you find the college or university, follow supporting links to a particular department or alumni association.

Stanford University—The Job Resource

http://solimar1.stanford.edu/prospects/search.html

Collection of resumes from graduates and undergraduates that attend or have recently attended various prestigious colleges from all over the world.

UCLA Alumweb

http://www.alumni.ucla.edu/index.cfm

Contains many links to home pages created by members of the UCLA Alumni Association.

Dr. Hansen's Student Home Pages, Stetson University's School of Business Administration, DeLand, Florida

http://www.stetson.edu/~rhansen/students.html

Provides links to current and former marketing students.

Industry-specific Web sites

Many individuals in both the liberal arts and computer-related fields are taking advantage of the Web to showcase their talent. Here are some interesting examples:

CareerMosaic AccountingNet—Accounting and Finance Jobs

http://www.accountingjobs.com

View resumes of college students and professionals seeking employment in the business and financial industries.

Chef's Express Resume Directory

http://www.chefsexpress.bc.ca/resume/cook.htm

View resumes of professional chefs and cooks.

HandiLinks to Resumes

http://www.ahandyguide.com

Enter the keyword "resumes" into the **Find** field in the upper left of the screen. This is a comprehensive resource for resumes that you can browse by industry. Navigating this site is somewhat cumbersome and may take awhile to initially upload, but the breadth of resumes might be just what you're looking for.

ResumeNet By Job Type

http://www.resumenet.com/byprof.html

View resumes in several different formats of high-tech professionals in the Silicon Valley (California) computer industry.

Resumes of Human Resource Professionals

http://www.pacificocean.com/hrguy/view.htm

View the resumes of human resource professionals, including contract corporate recruiters.

Saludos Web Resume Pool—Careers, Employment, Culture

http://www.saludos.com/resume.html

View resumes of qualified Hispanic professionals located in the United States seeking employment.

San Francisco Bay Area Independent Dance Teachers Directory

http://ballroom.com/resumes.htm

View resumes for area dance teachers, sponsored by Bill Rowe's Ballroom Dance Supply.

The Corporate Aviation Resume Exchange

http://scendtek.com/care

View the resumes of pilots. The resumes are indexed by location, flight hours, and aircraft licensed to fly.

Search engines

Search engines are the largest repositories of resumes and personal home pages posted by individuals. Many individuals submit the URL of their Web resume to a search engine, or they let the search engine find them via spiders. Spiders are automated software agents that "crawl" from URL to URL, and index the content of Web pages found. Instructions for optimizing your Web resume so recruiters can find you using search engines are provided in Chapter 10. For now, here are three popular search engines you can use to locate resumes online:

Alta Vista

http://www.altavista.digital.com

Search Alta Vista for thousands of resumes designed in plain HTML. This does not count resumes submitted to proprietary online resume databases. Search by keyword "resumes" to conduct a simple search.

Savvy Search

http://www.cs.colostate.edu/~dreiling/smartform.html

Simultaneously search by keywords and subject more than 20 search engines in 20 languages.

Yahoo!

http://www.yahoo.com

Search for resumes using the keywords "individual resume" and "seasonal resumes." One of the best collections of resumes listed by category for a wide variety of disciplines.

Lookup directories

Online yellow and white pages, business directories, and people finders are increasingly useful resources for finding resumes, since their emphasis is on finding people:

LookSmart

http://www.looksmart.com

Browse links to Personal Pages by surname, in alphabetical order, starting from the "People & Chat" link. Although these are primarily links to personal pages and direct links to resumes, it is a good way to see how people are integrating their resumes into other parts of their personal Web pages.

WhoWhere
http://www.whowhere.com

View resumes via WhoWhere's personal home page lookup, organized by category. For example, listed under the personal profiles category, you'll find links to resumes in a wide variety of professions, including administrative and business occupations, artists, clergy, entertainers, farmers, health care, legal occupations, personal care occupations, protective service occupations, and structural work occupations.

Who's Who On-Line, 3rd Edition, 1996
http://www.ictp.trieste.it/Canessa/ENTRIES/entries.html

Although this site is no longer maintained, there are still plenty of active links to resumes organized by profession and/or activity.

Internet service providers and Web hosting services

More places to find personal home pages and Web resumes are at sites where members can create free personal home pages. Many Internet Service Providers also offer free space to create Web pages with individual accounts. Here's a few you may wish to check out:

GeoCities
http://www.geocities.com

Search for resumes on the entire site, or narrow your search by keywords for a specific area of interest.

Teleport Internet Services
http://www.teleport.com

Browse community and member directories for links to personal home pages and pages by subject or category.

The List—The Definitive ISP Buyer's Guide
http://thelist.internet.com

Exhaustive directory listing more than 4,000 ISPs in the United States. Browse this directory to locate an ISP in your area. Visit some of their sites and browse their member home page directories.

Critiquing other resumes on the Web

Visiting Web resumes isn't sufficient. The key to success is to carefully analyze the strengths and weaknesses of each of the resumes you visit and keep track of your impressions and observations. Recording your impressions on a critique sheet can come in handy.

Complete a Web Resume Critique Sheet on page 99 for each resume you visit to guide the evaluation process. This makes it easy to evaluate the strengths and weaknesses of the important elements of each resume, as well as to provide a permanent record of the site visited, so you can refer to it later. Practice recording your initial impressions, and see how they might apply to your own resume. Learn to identify problem areas that you want to avoid when you create (or improve) your Web resume.

Following are some tips to help maximize your use of the Web Resume Critique Sheets, as well as your time online:

- Make several photocopies of the Critique Sheet and store them for handy reference.
- Include the date of your visit and the URL for each resume visited. Revisit the sample resumes periodically. If major changes have been made, note any important changes on the Critique Sheet. This is also a good opportunity to monitor other job-seekers online who take their Web resume offline because they found a job.
- Visit the best and worst resumes often, even if they have nothing to do with your industry. Your impressions of them may change as you gain more experience with the Web and your impressions become more refined.
- Make notes of how you found a particular resume. An advantage to seeking out other resumes on the Web is that you have the opportunity to investigate how a recruiter might find your resume once you post it.
- If the owner of the resume invites your feedback, feel free to comment. Be constructive or complimentary. The comments you provide will probably help when designing your own Web resume. Provide comments in a manner that you would feel comfortable receiving from others regarding your own site.
- Bookmark favorite resumes in your browser. Most Web browsers permit you to bookmark or copy the URL of the Web page you are viewing. Once you leave a Web page, it's nearly impossible to remember the URL. When you bookmark it, provide a meaningful name so you can remember something about it when you want to return to it.
- To bookmark Web pages in **Microsoft Internet Explorer:** Choose **Favorites | Add to Favorites....**
- To bookmark Web pages in **Netscape Communicator:** Choose **Communicator | Bookmarks | Add Bookmark.**

Take the time to visit the best and worst Web resumes often, using the critique exercise as an inspiration to maintain your own Web resume. Place Web resumes in context with your other career management options as they are most effective when integrated with other self-marketing. Your understanding of Web resumes as a job networking and career management tool places you at a competitive advantage over those who don't. The better your knowledge of Web-savvy resumes, and the better you employ it in your career search, the more successful you will be in the online career marketplace.

Web Resume Critique Sheet

Research the Web for examples of resumes and critique each of them by answering the following:

1. Web page URL (e.g., Web site address)?

2. Date visited?

3. What source did you use to find this Web page (search engine, friend, magazine, etc.)?

4. How quickly did the page load into your browser (describe)?

5. What were the first items to appear on the opening screen (e.g., text, images, etc.)?

6. Is the Web page visually attractive (e.g., background and text color, page layout)?

7. What kind of job do you think the job-seeker is looking for?

8. How easy is it to navigate through the Web page's information?

9. What did you find useful about this Web page? Why?

10. What did you find annoying about this Web page? Why?

11. What would you do to design this Web page differently? Why?

12. If you were a recruiter, would you feel compelled to contact this person?

Chapter 9

The Right Tools
for the Right Web Resume

The previous chapters in this book have showed you how to put together an electronically friendly resume. The next step in this process is to put your new resume onto the Web. If you want to know more, there are several learning resources listed in Appendices D and E. Although the exercises in this chapter use the Microsoft Internet Explorer Web browser for illustration, reference is made to the Netscape Communicator browser as a convenience where applicable.

In this chapter, you will learn how to:

• Create a Web resume from scratch using a text editor.
• Convert an existing resume into an HTML file using a word processor.
• Enhance a Web resume using a graphical HTML editor.

HTML editors

Your design depends upon the nature of the Web, the tools you use, and the Web browsers out on the market. To create Web pages, you need an HTML editor, a Web browser, and Internet access. HTML editors generally fall into the following three categories:

Text-based HTML Editors: Text editors require that you know HTML in sufficient detail to manually code HTML. Knowing the basics of raw HTML is like knowing basic auto mechanics. You have more creative flexibility when you manually insert HTML code. Typing the commands is often faster and easier than navigating through complex menus and dialog boxes. By learning to hand-code HTML, you are able to read and modify a Web page, no matter what tools were used to create it. Text-based HTML editors are on all PC and Macintosh computers as part of their operating system. The text editor included with the Mac OS is called SimpleText; the text editor included with Windows 95 and 98 is called Notepad.

Graphical HTML Editors: These editors combine the simplicity of word processors and editing capabilities of HTML text editors with a graphical user interface. They incorporate a Web browser that attempts to show the Web page with graphics and special formatting as you build it. The attraction of this type of editor is that you don't need to know HTML in order to create Web pages. Popular Web browsers now come bundled with graphical HTML editors as add-ons. Graphical HTML editors work entirely in HTML and require a basic knowledge of Web page design.

Two no-cost popular graphical HTML editors are FrontPage Express (included with the Microsoft Internet Explorer browser) and Netscape Composer (included with the Netscape Communicator browser). Download from:

- **Microsoft Internet Explorer:** http://www.microsoft.com/ie/download
- **Netscape Communicator:** http://www.netscape.com/download

Word Processors as Editors: Word processors are good to start with, considering most people know how to use them. Many of today's word-processing programs can save documents in HTML format.

The three most popular word processors are Microsoft Word, Corel WordPerfect, and Lotus WordPro. Microsoft Word 97 and 98 include the ability to open, edit, and save existing documents to HTML format, using the built-in Internet Assistant feature.

Older versions of word processors can be enhanced with add-ons for building Web pages. Microsoft has a version of Internet Assistant for Word 6.0a (or later) and Word95. The latest version of the Internet Assistant add-on is available as a free download from the c|net Web site (http://www.download.com). Search for it using the keywords "Internet Assistant."

Word 97 and 98 have sufficient basic HTML authoring support, making it easy to convert existing resume files into Web resumes, complete with backgrounds, graphic accents, images, links, and tables. In fact, if the resume includes table layouts, Word and Internet Assistant seamlessly translate them into HTML tables. However, Internet Assistant does not support building more advanced HTML capabilities, such as frames.

Creating a Web resume using Microsoft Notepad

The following exercises will show how to hand-code HTML using a standard text editor. However, before we get into that, you'll need to know the basic process of using your text editor as an HTML editor. The following steps are the basics for using your text editor as a powerful Web page creation tool:

1. Open the Windows Notepad text editor (or the Mac OS SimpleText editor).
2. Open the Microsoft Internet Explorer or Netscape Communicator Web browser.
3. Type HTML codes and text into the text editor to create a Web page.
4. Save the text editor document on the desktop.
5. Open this new file from the browser window to view your Web page as it would appear on the Web (Internet access is not required for these lessons).

6. Switch back to the text editor to type, edit, and save by clicking on its window to make it the active window.
7. Switch back to the browser to open the newly edited file by clicking on its window to make it the active window.
8. Update the document as it appears in the browser:

   • Microsoft Internet Explorer: Choose Refresh.
   • Netscape Communicator: Choose Reload.

Exercise 1: Setting up Web page document structure

As described in Chapter 8, an HTML document consists of text and tags. Converting a resume to HTML involves enclosing ASCII text with paired tags formatting information—the first tag turns on a formatting command—the second tag turns it off (indicated by the "/" within the angled brackets).

Every Web page contains the following basic structure:

```
<HTML>
<HEAD>
<TITLE> Resume of Thomas B. Seeker </TITLE>
<BODY>
[actual resume text]
</BODY>
</HEAD>
</HTML>
```

Tags can be typed in upper or lower case—they are *not* case sensitive. Most tags come in pairs, indicating "on" and "off" instructions. Some tags, such as
 (forces a new line), <LI> (indicates an item in a list), and <HR> (inserts a horizontal rule), are standalone tags. Tags and the text contained within them are called elements.

Exercise 1-1: Typing HTML tags

These steps introduce the document structure tags, which must be included in every Web page you create:

To set up your first Web page:
1. Open Microsoft Internet Explorer or Netscape Communicator browser.
2. Open the Notepad text editor. In Windows 95/98, Choose **Start | Programs | Accessories | Notepad**.
3. Type the following in the text editor:

```
<HTML>
<HEAD>
<TITLE> Resume of Thomas B. Seeker </TITLE>
</HEAD>
<BODY>
</BODY>
</HTML>
```

4. Save the file to the computer's desktop. Choose **File | Save As...**, then select `Desktop` as the destination folder. Enter `resume.html` as the file name. Choose **OK**.

5. Make the browser the active window by clicking it with the mouse. Resize the text editor and browser windows with the mouse so both fit on the screen for easy viewing. You will be switching back and forth between the two windows throughout these exercises.

6. Open the newly created `resume.html` file in the browser.

   - **Microsoft Internet Explorer:** Choose **File | Open... | Browse... | Desktop |** `resume.html` **| Open | OK**.
   - **Netscape Communicator: Choose File | Open... | Choose File... | Desktop |** `resume.html` **| Open | Open**.

Congratulations—you've just created your first page! As shown Figure 1, it does not look like much yet, but let's take a look at what you have. What you should see in the title bar is the text you typed between the <TITLE> tags in **Exercise 1-1**: `Resume of Thomas B. Seeker`.

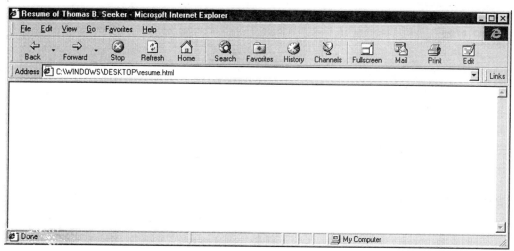

Figure 1. Results of this exercise thus far, as viewed in Microsoft Internet Explorer.

The opening and closing <TITLE> </TITLE> tags define what appears at the top of the browser in the title bar view when it loads the Web page, as shown in Figure 1. Title text identifies the name of a document to browsers, typically appearing in the browser's title bar (rather than in the document window). This is the text that appears in everyone's browser view when they visit your Web resume. It is also the text that is saved when visitors bookmark your Web resume in their browser, and the header and footer text that appears when they print your resume.

Give your page a title that clearly identifies its subject. Many search engines locate documents by <TITLE> </TITLE> tags. A generic title such as "My Home

Page" does not provide much information. Give your Web resume a title that clearly identifies its subject, such as "Resume of Thomas B. Seeker."

In addition, an HTML document must always start with <HTML> and end with </HTML>. These tags define everything in between as an HTML document.

The text within the <HEAD> </HEAD> tags is the Web page heading. The opening and closing <BODY> </BODY> tags indicate everything in between as the Web page's body.

To view the source HTML file contents, do the following:

- **Microsoft Internet Explorer:** Choose **View | Source**, as shown in Figure 2.
- **Netscape Communicator:** Choose **View | Page Source**.

You should now see the HTML code in your text editor's window. This is the HTML code you typed into your text editor earlier, as seen using the **View | Source** command from Microsoft Internet Explorer.

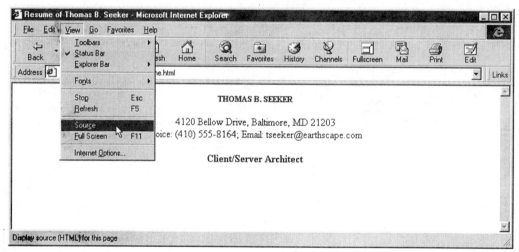

Figure 2. Flyout menu for viewing the source HTML file, as viewed in Microsoft Internet Explorer.

Exercise 1-2: Typing text—Contact information

To display body text in the Web resume:

1. Make the text editor the active window by clicking on it with the mouse.
2. Type the following four lines of text in the text editor window, after the <BODY> tag. Separate each line by hitting ENTER at the end of each line. Add an extra carriage return before "Client/Server Architect."

```
THOMAS B. SEEKER
4120 Bellow Drive, Baltimore, MD 21203
Voice: (410) 555-8164; E-mail: tseeker@earthscape.com
Client/Server Architect
```

3. Choose **File | Save** to save the document.
4. Switch back to the browser window and update the document.

 - **Microsoft Internet Explorer:** Choose **Refresh**.
 - **Netscape Communicator:** Choose **Reload**.

You should now see the three sentences that you typed, in one continuous line of text. The layout used while typing the document in the text editor does not affect the results in the browser. You could type the following without changing the result:

```
<HTML><HEAD><TITLE> Resume of Thomas B. Seeker </TITLE>
</HEAD> <BODY>
THOMAS B. SEEKER
4120 Bellow Drive, Baltimore, MD 21203
Voice: (410) 555-8164; E-mail: tseeker@earthscape.com
Client/Server Architect
</BODY></HTML>
```

Exercise 1-3: Controlling line endings

To control line endings and vertical space, it is necessary to use specific line-ending tags. The <P> </P> tag pair inserts a blank line above and below the enclosed text. The <BR> tag forces a line break, but does not insert a blank line.

To force line breaks after each line of text in the information heading:

1. Make the text editor the active window by clicking it with the mouse.
2. Type <BR> at the end of the first three lines of text. For example:

```
THOMAS B. SEEKER <BR>
4120 Bellow Drive, Baltimore, MD 21203 <BR>
Voice: (410) 555-8164; E-mail: tseeker@earthscape.com <BR>
Client/Server Architect
```

3. Choose **File | Save**.
4. Switch back to the browser window and update the document as it appears in your browser. Note how each line of text now appears on its own line.

To separate the text into two separate paragraphs:

1. Make the text editor the active window by clicking it with the mouse.
2. Enclose the last line of text within <P></P> tags. For example:

```
<P>Client/Server Architect </P>
```

At this point, the text should resemble the following:

```
<HTML> <HEAD> <TITLE> Resume of Thomas B. Seeker </TITLE>
</HEAD> <BODY>
THOMAS B. SEEKER <BR>
4120 Bellow Drive, Baltimore, MD 21203 <BR>
Voice: (410) 555-8164; E-mail: tseeker@earthscape.com <BR>
<P>Client/Server Architect</P>
</BODY></HTML>
```

3. Choose **File | Save**.
4. Switch back to the browser window and update the document as it appears in the browser. Note the new space that appears after the e-mail address and before the words "Client/Server Architect."

Exercise 1-4: Aligning text

To align paragraph text to the center of the page, use the ALIGN="CENTER" attribute and variable within a <P> tag. Attributes are formatting instructions used within an HTML tag to control exactly what the tag does. Variables are instructions that modify the attributes, often appearing within quotation marks. For example, in order to align text to the right or left, you would use ALIGN="RIGHT" or ALIGN="LEFT".

To horizontally align information to the center of the page:

1. Make the text editor the active window by clicking it with the mouse.
2. Enclose the first three lines of text between the <P> </P> tags. Use the ALIGN="CENTER" attribute. The closing </P> tag should replace the <BR> tag.

```
<P ALIGN="CENTER"> THOMAS B. SEEKER <BR>
4120 Bellow Drive, Baltimore, MD 21203 <BR>
Voice: (410) 555-8164; E-mail: tseeker@earthscape.com </P>
```

3. Center the job title text by adding the ALIGN="CENTER" attribute to the text:

```
<P ALIGN="CENTER"> Client/Server Architect </P>
```

4. Choose **File | Save**.
5. Switch back to the browser window and update the document as it appears in your browser. Note the text is now centered and spaced similarly to the text created in **Exercise 1-3**.

Exercise 1-5: Emphasizing text with boldface type

To emphasize text with boldface type:

1. Make the text editor the active window.
2. Enclose the name and job title text within the <B></B> tag pair.

```
<P ALIGN="CENTER"> <B> THOMAS B. SEEKER </B> <BR>
4120 Bellow Drive, Baltimore, MD 21203 <BR>
Voice: (410) 555-8164; E-mail: tseeker@earthscape.com </P>
<P ALIGN="CENTER"> <B> Client/Server Architect </B> </P>
```

3. Choose **File | Save**.
4. Switch back to the browser window and update the document as it appears in your browser. The name and job title now appear in bold typeface.

Exercise 2: Headings

The six levels of HTML headings (<H1> through <H6>) are used to create an outline structure to your Web page (see Figure 3). They can also be used instead of bolding or changing the size of type.

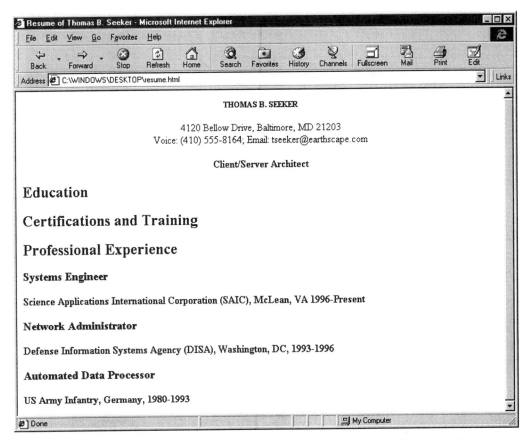

Figure 3. The effects of heading tags on text, as viewed in Internet Explorer.

Heading tags do not use the <P> </P> tag pair, as they are assumed to be a paragraph. They also do not require use of the <BR> tag at the end of a heading line. You may, however, use <BR> to break lines within the heading. The <B> </B> tag pair is also not necessary, as headings automatically appear bolded.

This exercise demonstrates the use of heading tags. Although <H1> </H1> is typically the first tag pair used in an outline, we are using subhead level <H5> </H5>, so that the name on the resume does not appear overly large.

To apply headings to the Web resume:

1. Enclose the name within the <H5> </H5> tag pair. Use the <CENTER> </CENTER> tag pair to center the first three lines of text.

```
<CENTER>
<H5>THOMAS B. SEEKER </H5>
4120 Bellow Drive, Baltimore, MD 21203 <BR>
Voice: (410) 555-8164; E-mail: tseeker@earthscape.com </P>
</CENTER>
```

2. Type the following heading in the text editor, beginning on a new line after the job title text entered in **Exercise 1**. Use <H2> </H2> with each heading.

```
<H2> Education </H2>
<H2> Certifications and Training </H2>
<H2> Professional Experience </H2>
```

3. For the heading "Professional Experience," type three job titles held, using `<H3>` `</H3>` with each job title.

```
<H3> Systems Engineer </H3>
<H3> Network Administrator </H3>
<H3> Automated Data Processor </H3>
```

4. Save the changes and preview them in the browser.
5. After each job title, type three subordinate headings that list the employer and dates employed. Use `<H4>` `</H4>` with each employer listed.

```
<H3> Systems Engineer </H3>
<H4> Science Applications International Corporation (SAIC),
McLean, VA, 1996-Present </H4>
<H3> Network Administrator </H3>
<H4> Defense Information Systems Agency (DISA), Washington, DC,
1993-1996 </H4>
<H3> Automated Data Processor </H3>
<H4> US Army Infantry, Germany, 1980-1993 </H4>
```

6. Save the changes and preview them in your browser as shown in Figure 3.

Exercise 3: Lists

List tags provide a different way of organizing data than headings. They are especially important in organizing your work and education experience in your e-resume. Look at Figure 4 to see how HTML lists can work for you.

In HTML, there are three types of lists you can use:

• An ordered list or numbered list, using the `<OL>` `</OL>` tag pair.
• An unordered or bulleted list, using the `<UL>` `</UL>` tag pair.
• A multilevel list, created by nesting the `<OL>` `</OL>` and `<UL>` `</UL>` tags.

When items are added to or subtracted from an ordered list, the list automatically renumbers itself.

All three types of lists use the `<LI>` tag, which specifies a single list item on the list and breaks the line between items. Like the `<BR>` tag, the `<LI>` tag stands by itself, without need for a closing tag.

Exercise 3-1: Unordered (bulleted) lists—Certifications and Training

To create an unordered (bulleted) list under a heading:

1. Type the following text under the heading, "Certifications and Training:"

```
Microsoft Certified Systems Engineer (MCSE #132546), August, 1997
Microsoft Certified Product Specialist, TCP/IP Networking, June, 1997
Transmission Control Protocol/Internet Protocol (TCP/IP),
Technology Systems Institute, 1996
```

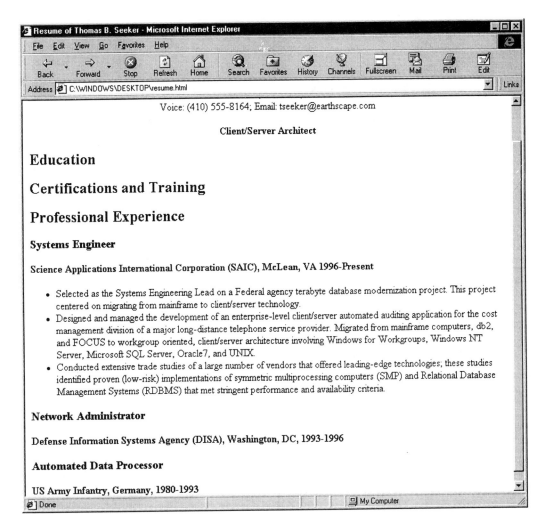

Figure 4. An unordered list using HTML `<LI>` and `<UL>` tags.

```
Database  Administration,  Performance  Tuning,  and  Benchmarking
with Oracle7, Oracle Corporation, 1995
Computer  Systems  Technology  Program,  Air  Force  Institute  of
Technology (AFIT), Graduate Courses in Software Engineering and
Computer Communications (24 quarter units completed), 1992
```

2. Insert `<UL>` at the top of the list to indicate the beginning of an unordered, or bulleted, list. Next, begin each list item with `<LI>`. End the list with `</UL>`.

```
<UL>
<LI> Microsoft Certified Systems Engineer (MCSE #132546), August, 1997
<LI> Microsoft Certified Product Specialist, TCP/IP Networking, June,
1997
<LI>  Transmission  Control  Protocol/Internet  Protocol  (TCP/IP),
Technology Systems Institute, 1996
<LI> Database Administration, Performance Tuning, and Benchmarking
with Oracle7, Oracle Corporation, 1995
```

```
<LI> Computer Systems Technology Program, Air Force Institute of
Technology (AFIT), Graduate Courses in Software Engineering and
Computer Communications (24 quarter units completed), 1992
</UL>
```

3. Save the changes and preview them in your browser.

Exercise 3-2: Unordered (bulleted) lists—Professional experience

To create a bulleted list for each job held:

1. After one of the employer's headings created in **Exercise 2** (for example, "Science Applications International Corporation [SAIC]"), insert <UL> to indicate the beginning of an unordered list (as you did in **Exercise 3-1**). Using <LI>, list the accomplishments for that job, then end the list with </UL>.

```
<H4> Science Applications International Corporation (SAIC),
McLean, VA 1996-Present </H4>
<UL>
<LI>Selected as Systems Engineering Lead on a federal agency
terabyte database modernization project. This project centered on
migrating from mainframe to client/server technology.</LI>
<LI>Designed and managed the development of an enterprise-level
client/server automated auditing application for the cost
management division of a major long-distance telephone service
provider. Migrated from mainframe computers, db2, and FOCUS to
workgroup-oriented, client/server architecture involving Windows
for Workgroups, Windows NT Server, Microsoft SQL Server, Oracle7,
and UNIX.</LI>
</UL>
```

2. Save the changes and preview them in your browser.
3. Create an unordered list of accomplishments for the remaining job titles, then save the changes and preview them in your browser, as shown in Figure 4.

Exercise 4: Links

Three kinds of linking actions can be initiated (refer to Figure 5):

1. Linking to a different location in the same Web page by way of a bookmark (reference to a location within the same Web page).
2. Linking to another Web page located in the same directory by way of its filename.
3. Linking to another Web page located on the Web by way of its URL.

Links can be text or graphics. To access the link, users choose the highlighted text or graphic. In Microsoft Internet Explorer or Netscape Communicator, links usually appear underlined and in a different color. Linked graphics typically have a colored box around them. The mouse pointer changes into a pointing finger or other user-defined icon passed over a link. After choosing a text link, the text color changes to indicate its recent use. The reminder usually lasts about 30 days.

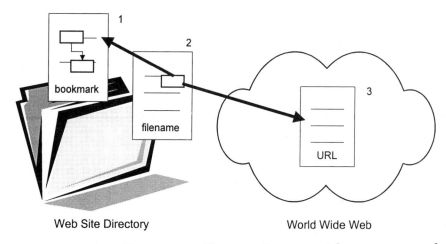

Web Site Directory   World Wide Web

Figure 5. Hyperlinks allow your audience to interact with your page and connect to other pages.

Various link characteristics (such as color and length of time the browser remembers it as a used link) are user-defined in the browser preference settings. Preference settings are accessible as follows:

- **Microsoft Internet Explorer: View | Internet Options...**
- **Netscape Communicator: Edit | Preferences...**

The tag pair used for creating anchors—hyperlink reference points—is `<A> </A>`. This paired tag has two attributes, `HREF` and `NAME`.

`HREF` (Hypertext Reference) specifies a Web page or location within a Web page to display once the link is selected. The text that appears with `HREF` appears within quotation marks. This text is not case sensitive unless it refers to a file name or bookmark anchor. The text that appears within the `<A> </A>` tag pair is the text users click to jump to the new destination. For example:

- `<A HREF="http://www.eresumes.com"> Click here! </A>`
- `See <A HREF="http://www.eresumes.com/tut_eresume.html"> to find out what E-Rez sez about choosing your best eResume format </A>`
- `<A HREF="#Experience"> Professional Experience </A>`
- `<A HREF="photo.html#PhotoThomas"> Thomas B. Seeker </A>`

`NAME` creates an anchor to a destination within a Web page. The word that appears with `NAME` appears within quotes and is case sensitive. Use any word as the anchor name, but choose a word that relates to the linked text. Anchor names within the same page must be unique. There is no limit to the number of links that can point at the same `NAME` anchor. The text that appears within the `<A> </A>` tags is the text users see at the new destination. For example:

`<A NAME="Experience"> Professional Experience </A>`

File names and anchor names are case sensitive. If you name an anchor "Experience" instead of "experience" be sure that the hyperlink reference is spelled and capitalized the same way. To ensure case consistency, copy and paste the anchor name to the text used in the HREF link or bookmark.

Exercise 4-1: Linking to a destination within the same Web page

To link to other text or graphics in the same Web page, first create an anchor with the NAME attribute that identifies the particular text or graphic to which you want to link. Then, you need to create a hypertext reference to the anchor with HREF.

To link to text or graphics within the same Web page:

1. Make resume.html the active document in the text editor.
2. Scroll to the heading, "Professional Experience." Place the cursor after the <H2> tag, then enter the opening and closing anchor tag pair, as follows:

   ```
   <A NAME="Experience"> Professional Experience </A>
   ```

   The text should now resemble the following:

   ```
   <H2> <A NAME="Experience"> Professional Experience </A> </H2>
   ```

3. Scroll to just before the job title text, "Client/Server Architect," at the beginning of the resume document.
4. Place the cursor after the <B> tag, then enclose the job title within the hyperlink reference text, as follows:

   ```
   <A HREF="#Experience"> Client/Server Architect </A>
   ```

   The text should now resemble the following:

   ```
   <P  ALIGN="CENTER">  <B>  <A  HREF="#Experience">  Client/Server
   Architect </A> </B> </P>
   ```

   The # symbol identifies the hypertext reference as a link to a bookmark. The bookmark anchor text is case sensitive and must be entered *exactly* as it appears at the NAME location.

5. Save the changes and preview them in your browser.
6. Test the link. If the tags are entered correctly, "Client/Server Architect" indicates it is a hypertext link. When this link is chosen, the browser looks for the Experience bookmark on the Web page, and finds the "Professional Experience" text.

Exercise 4-2: Linking between Web pages within the same Web site

When creating a link from one Web page to another within the same Web site, it is not necessary to specify a complete URL. Instead, you simply specify the filename. For example:

- <A HREF="photo.html"> Thomas B. Seeker </A> points to the photo.html file in the same folder as the current Web page

- `<A HREF="photo.html#PhotoThomas">` Thomas B. Seeker `</A>` points to the anchor Photo Thomas in the `photo.html` file, in the same folder as the current Web page
- `<A HREF="images/photo.jpg">` Thomas B. Seeker `</A>` points to the `photo.jpg` file in the images folder of the current Web site.

To link between Web pages within the same Web site:

1. Use the text editor to create a new file called `photo.html`, then save it to the Desktop folder (the same folder in which you saved the `resume.html` file).
2. Set up the page's structure tags by typing the following into the text editor:

```
<HTML>
<HEAD>
<TITLE> Photo of Thomas B. Seeker </TITLE>
</HEAD>
<BODY>
</BODY>
</HTML>
```

3. Save the changes and preview them in the browser.
4. Open `resume.html` in the text editor.
5. Scroll to the top of the page. Enclose the name "Thomas B. Seeker" within the hyperlink reference text, as follows:

```
<A HREF="photo.html"> Thomas B. Seeker </A>
```

The text should now resemble the following:

```
<H5> <A HREF="photo.html"> Thomas B. Seeker </A> </H5>
```

6. Save `resume.html` in the text editor and preview the changes in the browser. If you typed the anchor tag link element correctly, "Thomas B. Seeker" appears as a link, underlined and in a different color.
7. Choose the link. The browser displays the `photo.html` document. If your link doesn't work, make sure the `resume.html` and the `photo.html` files are in the same file folder.

Exercise 4-3: Linking to another Web page located on another Web site

Linking to another Web site follows the same procedure as linking to another location within the same Web site. However, it is necessary to provide the entire Internet address of the destination site. Because URLs must be entered *exactly*, you may find it easier to copy and paste URLs rather than typing them.

To copy and paste, select the URL that you want to copy. Choose **Edit | Copy**, go to the place where you want to paste the URL, then choose **Edit | Paste**.

To create a link to another Web site:

1. Make `resume.html` the active document in the text editor.
2. Scroll to the words "Science Applications International Corporation (SAIC)."

3. Place the cursor after the <H4> tag, then enclose the company name within the hyperlink reference text, as follows:

    ```
    <A    HREF="http://www.saic.alaska.net">   Science   Applications
    International Corporation (SAIC) </A>
    ```

    The text should now resemble the following:

    ```
    <H4> <A HREF="http://www.saic.alaska.net"> Science Applications
    International Corporation (SAIC)</A>, McLean, VA 1996-Present
    </H4>
    ```

4. Save the changes and preview them in the browser. If you typed the anchor tag link element correctly, "Science Applications International Corporation (SAIC)" appears as a link (underlined and in a different color).
5. To test this link, it is necessary to connect to the Internet. When you click the link, the browser instructs the server to load the document located at the following URL: http://www.saic.alaska.net.

Exercise 5: Images

Graphics are stored in separate files, as referenced in the HTML code for a Web page with the <IMG> tag and the SRC attribute (which identifies the source file of the image). They can also be used as background images, as part of the <BODY> tag, <BODY BACKGROUND="IMAGE.JPG">. For a review on image file formats, see Chapter 4.

Exercise 5-1: Inserting an image into a Web page

To create an image file, scan it yourself if you have the equipment. If you don't have a scanner, use a service like that provided by Kinko's to scan a photograph of yourself, convert it to the appropriate file format, and copy it onto a floppy disk. Then it is just a matter of transferring that file into the same folder in which you are storing your Web page files. Let's assume you have done this, and now have a file called photo.jpg.

To insert an image into a Web page:

1. Make the text editor the active window.
2. Open the photo.html file created in **Exercise 4-2**.
3. Insert the following element tag between the <BODY> </BODY> tag pair. Enclose the name of the image file with quotations marks, as shown:

    ```
    <IMG SRC="photo.jpg">
    ```

4. The text should now resemble the following:

    ```
    <BODY>
    <IMG SRC="photo.jpg">
    </BODY>
    ```

5. The <IMG SRC=> tag instructs the browser to load the image file photo.jpg, located in the same folder as the photo.html file.

6. Save the changes and preview them in your browser. The photograph you scanned earlier with the file name `photo.jpg` should appear in the browser window (see Figure 6). If the image does not appear, check that the `photo.html` and `photo.jpg` files are located in the same folder; and the file name is the same one that appears on your hard drive.

Figure 6. The `photo.html` should show your photo, similar to the one above for Thomas B. Seeker.

Exercise 5-2: Capturing and inserting an image

Another way of acquiring images to add to your Web page is to copy or "capture" them from another page located somewhere else on the Web, and store them onto your local hard drive. To complete this next series of steps, you must be connected to the Internet.

To capture and insert an image:

1. Make the browser the active window.
2. Go to a Web page that has a graphic you want. Type its URL in the **Address** field (`http://www.microsoft.com/gallery/images/default.asp,` for example).
3. Choose **Show Contents**. An expandable list of contents appears.
4. Choose a content category to view ("Buttons," for example).
5. Choose an image to view (for example, "Pencil and Paper").
6. Activate the shortcut menu to copy the image.

- **Windows:** Press and hold the secondary mouse button (typically the right mouse button) over the image until the pop-up menu appears.
- **Macintosh:** Press and hold the mouse button over the image until the pop-up menu appears.

7. Save the image to the Desktop folder (the same folder in which you saved the photo.html file). Keep the same file extension, .gif or .jpg, as the original image (for example, icon_pencil.gif).

   - **Microsoft Internet Explorer:** Choose **Save Picture As...**, change to the Desktop folder, then choose **Save**.
   - **Netscape Communicator:** Choose **Save Image As...**, change to the Desktop folder, then choose **Save**.

8. Open the photo.html file in the text editor.
9. Insert the following element tag anywhere between the <BODY> </BODY> tag pair. Enclose the name of the image file within quotations marks, as shown:

   ```
   <IMG SRC="icon_pencil.gif">
   ```

   Be sure to add a space between the two <IMG SRC=> tags. The text block should now resemble the following:

   ```
   <BODY>
   <IMG SRC="photo.jpg"> <IMG SRC="icon_pencil.gif">
   </BODY>
   ```

   The <IMG SRC=> tag tells the browser to load the file icon_pencil.gif, located in the same folder as the photo.html file.
10. Save the changes and preview them in the browser. The image should appear next to the photo in your document.
11. To place images one on top of the other, add one or two <BR> tags between the two <IMG SRC=> tags to add a space between them. For example:

    ```
    <BODY> <IMG SRC="photo.jpg"> <BR> <BR> <IMG SRC="icon_pencil.jpg">
    </BODY>
    ```
12. Do not capture images from other Web pages unless they are public domain, or you have permission from their owner. Capturing images without permission is in potential violation of copyright.

Exercise 5-3: Capturing and assigning a background image

Adding a background image to your page will give your e-resume a more professional and pleasing look (see Figure 7). To display a background image, you will use the BACKGROUND="image.jpg" attribute and variable within the <BODY> tag.

To capture and assign a background image:

1. Make the browser the active window.
2. Load a Web page that has a background graphic you want to capture. Type the WebpageURL in the **Address** field of the browser.

Figure 7. The `photo.html` file, now with a background image inserted behind the photo.

3. Choose **Show Contents**. An expandable list of contents appears.
4. Choose a content category to view (for example, "Backgrounds").
5. Choose an image to view (for example, "Blue Marble").
6. Activate the shortcut menu to copy the image.

   - **Windows:** Press and hold the secondary mouse button (typically the right-mouse button) over the image until the pop-up menu appears.
   - **Macintosh:** Press and hold the mouse button over the image until the pop-up menu appears.

7. Save the image to the Desktop folder (the same folder in which you saved the `photo.html` file). Keep the same file extension, `.jpg`, as the original image (for example, `b_rock.jpg`).

   - **Microsoft Internet Explorer:** Choose **Save Picture As...**, change to the Desktop folder, then choose **Save**.
   - **Netscape Communicator:** Choose **Save Image As...**, change to the Desktop folder, then choose **Save**.

8. Open the `photo.html` file in the text editor.
9. Insert the following attribute and variable within the `<BODY>` tag. Enclose the name of the image file within quotations marks, as shown:

   ```
   <BODY BACKGROUND="b_rock.jpg">
   ```

The text block should now resemble the following:

```
<BODY BACKGROUND="b_rock.jpg">
<IMG SRC="photo.jpg"> <IMG SRC="icon_pencil.gif"> </BODY>
```

The `BACKGROUND="b_rock.jpg"` attribute and variable instruct the browser to load the image file `b_rock.jpg`, located in the same folder as the `photo.html` file, behind the text and images in the body of the Web page.

10. Save the changes and preview them in the browser (see Figure 8). The image should appear in the background of the document.

Creating a Web Resume using Microsoft FrontPage Express

For some, hand-coding HTML can be a tedious process using text-based HTML text editors such as Notepad. A WYSIWYG editor, such as FrontPage Express, allows you to automate this process.

Microsoft provides FrontPage Express free with Internet Explorer 4.0. FrontPage Express is a scaled-down version of the full-featured HTML editor, Microsoft FrontPage. It has menus and buttons that allow you to bold text, change font size, and execute more HTML-specific commands. Because it has a solid set of HTML features and includes a WYSIWYG interface, FrontPage Express is a good tool for editing or creating Web resumes.

To obtain Microsoft Internet Explorer:

- Download the platform version for your operating system from the Microsoft Web site: `http://www.microsoft.com/ie/global/newprodpop.htm`
- Purchase the installation CD online for about $7.00 at the Microsoft Web site: `http://ie4cd.microsoft.com/gintl_country.asp`

When you created the sample resume earlier in this chapter, you saw only text and formatting tags. With a graphical editor, you do not see the tags. Instead, you see text, displayed much like a word processor. You can mark text using different styles, which beneath the surface create HTML tags for headings, paragraphs, bulleted lists, and other types of markup language.

The difference between using Word and FrontPage Express is that FrontPage Express provides advanced HTML, such as images, video, background sounds, WebBot components (tools for adding timestamps, search boxes, and other Web items), ActiveX controls, Java Applets, plug-ins, and PowerPoint animations. When used in tandem with hard-coding, you will be a master at creating your own Web pages.

To access FrontPage Express after installing it onto your computer:

- Open FrontPage Express directly (part of the Internet Explorer program suite) to create a new file.
- Choose **Edit | Page** from within Internet Explorer to edit the currently displayed Web page.

Exercise 6: Creating a new file

Although hard-coding HTML is best, FrontPage Express can significantly ease the burden of creating your Web resume. All the required HTML tags you entered manually in **Exercise 1** are automatically created by FrontPage Express when you create a new file.

Figure 8 shows the default FrontPage Express window, with callouts for common tools and information.

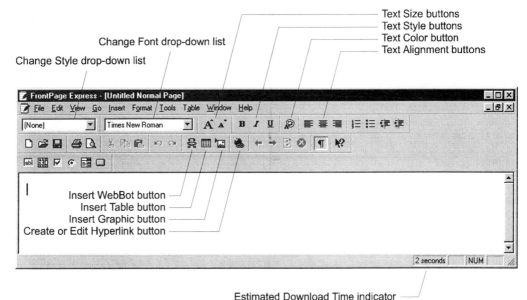

Figure 8. Default FrontPage Express window.

Exercise 6-1: Creating the basic HTML text

To create the basic HTML text for the new Web resume file

1. Open FrontPage Express.
2. Choose **View | HTML....** You should see the HTML code for the document structure, automatically inserted by FrontPage Express (it is not necessary to type it manually, as you did in **Exercise 1** earlier in this chapter). You should also see a new set of tags called <META> tags, which are discussed in more detail in Chapter 10. Notice the default text, "Untitled Normal Page" within the <TITLE> </TITLE> tag pair, as shown in Figure 9. You can edit this text in the **View or Edit HTML** window.
3. Choose **OK** to return to the main FrontPage Express window.
4. Choose **File | Save**.
5. Type "Resume of Thomas B. Seeker" in the **Page Title** field. The text you enter is automatically inserted within <TITLE> </TITLE>. Ignore the text in the **Page Location** field.
6. Choose **As File....**

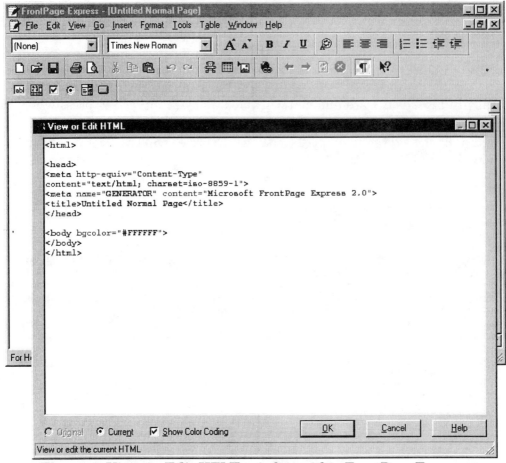

Figure 9. View or Edit HTML window within FrontPage Express.

7. Select a folder in which to save this file (the Desktop folder where the files were saved in the previous exercises, for example), then type `resume2.html` in the **Filename:** field. Ensure that **Save as type** is **HTML Files** (`*.htm`, `*.html`), then choose **Save**.

8. Once the file is saved, load it into Internet Explorer to see how it looks.

To view the changes in Microsoft Internet Explorer:

1. Start Internet Explorer.
2. Choose **File | Open**, enter the path of the Web page to view, then choose **OK**.
3. Choose the **Refresh** button in the Internet Explorer toolbar to view changes saved to the file in FrontPage Express.

Exercise 6-2: Entering text

The following steps demonstrate how to enter text directly into FrontPage Express without typing the HTML tags. Using FrontPage Express is very easy. All you need to do is enter your Web page's text in the same way you would type a letter in a word processor!

To enter text in a Web resume:

1. Make FrontPage Express the active window by clicking it with the mouse.
2. Enter the following four lines of text. Add soft returns (press SHIFT + ENTER) at the end of the first two lines. Add carriage returns (press ENTER) at the end of the third and fourth lines:

```
THOMAS B. SEEKER
4120 Bellow Drive, Baltimore, MD 21203
Voice: (410) 555-8164; E-mail: tseeker@earthscape.com
Client/Server Architect
```

3. Choose **File | Save** to save the document. Notice what happens when you press ENTER after typing the e-mail address. FrontPage Express will automatically create an e-mail hyperlink. This is set off from the other text by making the e-mail address underlined and in a different color. This can be seen in Figure 10.

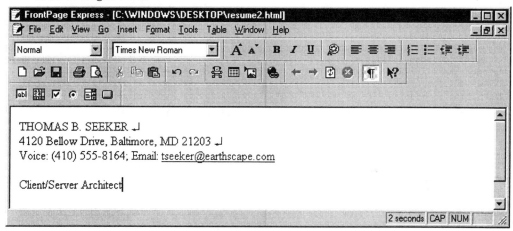

Figure 10. FrontPage Express window with contact information text.

4. Switch back to the browser window and update the document as it appears in the browser. What you saw in FrontPage Express should also be what you now see in Internet Explorer.
5. Choose **View | HTML...** to see the raw HTML code, as in Figure 11.

Exercise 6-3: Controlling line endings

How you enter line breaks in FrontPage Express determines how text appears in the Web browser.

Press ENTER to make the current text a paragraph, followed by a blank line. FrontPage Express inserts <P> at the beginning of the paragraph text and </P> at the end of the paragraph text.

Press SHIFT + ENTER to create a soft return and continue the current text on the following line, with no blank line in between. FrontPage Express inserts <BR> at the end of the line of text.

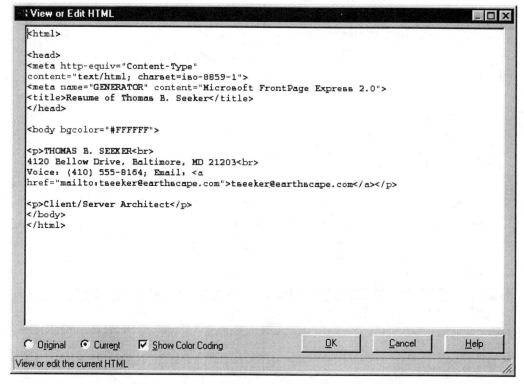

Figure 11. Results so far in the **View or Edit HTML** window.

Exercise 7: Formatting text

Formatting text in FrontPage Express is a snap. All you need to use are the formatting buttons in the toolbar, as shown previously in Figure 8.

Exercise 7-1: Aligning text

To center selected text:

1. Place the cursor on the "Thomas B. Seeker" text.
2. Press and hold the primary mouse button, then move the mouse to highlight and select the "Thomas B. Seeker" and "Client/Server Architect" text. Release the mouse button.
3. Choose the Align Center button on the toolbar. The text is automatically centered. When viewing the HTML, you'll notice that <P ALIGN="CENTER"> appears at the beginning of the "Thomas B. Seeker" and "Client/Server Architect" text (see Figure 12).
4. Save your changes.

Exercise 7-2: Headings

Use headings to create subcategories of text, such as education, job experience and accomplishments, and so forth.

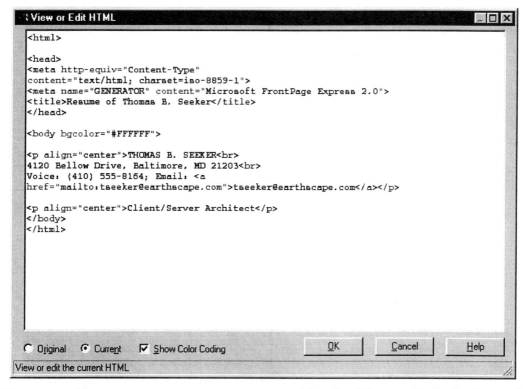

Figure 12. The `<p align="CENTER">` tag used for the "Thomas B. Seeker" and the "Client/Server Architect" text.

To format headings:

1. Beginning on a new line after the "Client/Server Architect" text, enter these three headings in FrontPage Express. Press ENTER after each heading:

```
Professional Experience
Systems Engineer
Science Applications International Corporation (SAIC), McLean, VA
1996-Present
```

2. Select all three lines of text you just entered, then choose the Left Align button in the toolbar.
3. Place the cursor on the first heading, "Professional Experience," then choose Heading 2 from the **Change Style** drop-down list.
4. Place the cursor on the second heading, "Systems Engineer." Choose Heading 3 from the **Change Style** drop-down list.
5. Place the cursor on the third heading, "Science Applications." Choose Heading 4 from the **Change Style** drop-down list.
6. Notice the differences between each heading. When viewed with **View | HTML...**, each heading is now in its own heading tag pair (see Figure 13).
7. Save the changes.
8. Repeat this exercise for other major headings and subheadings to be listed in the sample resume.

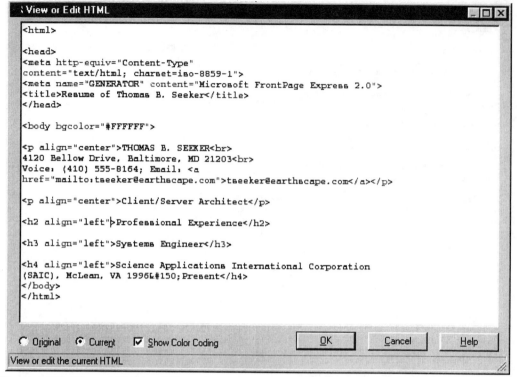

Figure 13. The addition of the `<H# ALIGN=LEFT> </H#>` tag pairs for the heading text.

Exercise 7-3: Bulleted lists

Use bullets to create lists of information, such as accomplishments and education information.

To create a bulleted list of accomplishments for the "Science Applications..." heading:

1. Enter the following text, beginning on a new line after the employer heading, "Science Applications." Press ENTER at the end of each text block:

    Selected as the Systems Engineering Lead on a Federal agency terabyte database modernization project. This project centered on migrating from mainframe to client/server technology.

    Designed and managed the development of an enterprise-level client/server automated auditing application for the cost management division of a major long-distance telephone service provider. Migrated from mainframe computers, db2, and FOCUS to workgroup-oriented, client/server architecture involving Windows for Workgroups, Windows NT Server, Microsoft SQL Server, Oracle7, and UNIX.

    Conducted extensive trade studies of a large number of vendors that offered leading-edge technologies; these studies identified proven (low-risk) implementations of symmetric multiprocessing computers (SMP) and Relational Database

Management Systems (RDBMS) that met stringent performance and availability criteria.

2. Place the cursor on the "Selected as" text.
3. Press and hold the primary mouse button, then move the mouse to highlight the "Selected as" and "Designed and managed" text. Release the button.
4. Choose "Bulleted List" from the **Change Style** drop-down list. The text blocks are now bulleted. When viewed with **View | HTML...**, each text block is now preceded by <LI>. The entire list is enclosed between <UL> </UL>.
5. Save your changes (see Figure 14).
6. Repeat this exercise for the accomplishments to be listed with the remaining employer headings in the sample resume.
7. Repeat this exercise for other lists, such as the "Education" and "Certification and Training" headings in the sample resume.

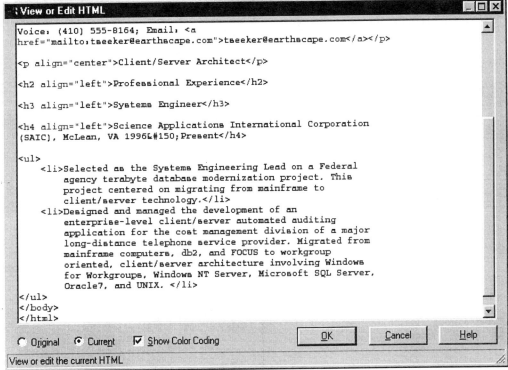

Figure 14. Note the addition of the <UL> </UL> and <LI> tags for the list text.

Exercise 8: Links

Links are easy to create and keep track of in FrontPage Express.

Exercise 8-1: Bookmark links

You can easily add a hyperlink to a page using the **Insert | Hyperlink** command. Using bookmarks, you can easily link to any place on the target page.

To add a bookmark to the resume:

1. Select the words "Professional Experience," then choose **Edit | Bookmark....** The Bookmark dialog box appears.
2. Enter a name for the bookmarked location in the **Bookmark Name:** field (such as "Experience" or "Professional Experience"), then choose **OK**. The bookmarked text now appears with a broken underscore (see Figure 15).
3. Scroll to the beginning of the resume document, highlight and select the words "Client/Server Architect," then choose **Insert | Hyperlink....**
4. Choose the **Open Pages** tab, then select "Resume of Thomas B. Seeker."
5. Select "Experience" from the **Bookmark** drop-down list, then choose **OK** (see Figure 16). The hyperlinked text is now underlined.
6. Save the changes. Switch back to the browser window and update the document as it appears in the browser.
7. Click on the link to test it.. If the tags were entered correctly, "Client/Server Architect" will indicate that it is a hypertext link. When this link is chosen, the browser will look for the "Experience" bookmark on your Web page, and find the "Professional Experience" text. When viewed in the **View | HTML...** window, `<a href="#Experience"> </a>` will enclose the "Client/Server Architect" text and `<a name="Experience"> </a>` will enclose the "Professional Experience" text.

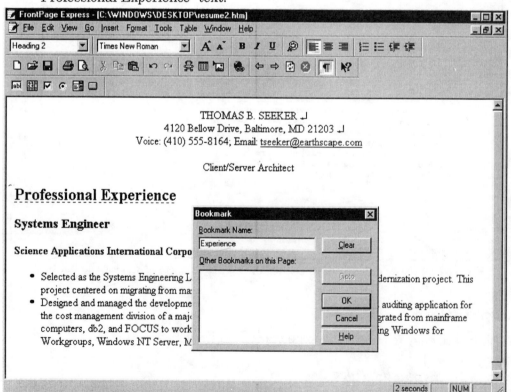

Figure 15. FrontPage Express, shown with the **Bookmark** dialog box and the result of adding the bookmark, as applied to the "Professional Experience" text.

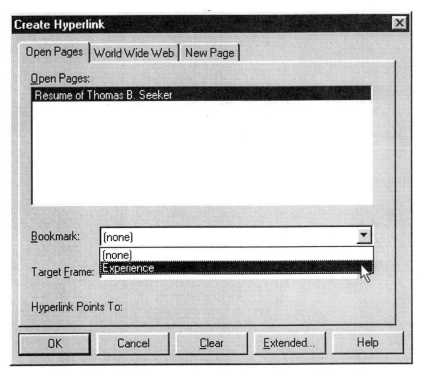

Figure 16. Select "Resume of Thomas B. Seeker," then select "Experience" from the **Bookmark** drop-down list.

Exercise 8-2: Local links

You can easily link to another page located in the same folder or path. This exercise makes use of the `photo.html` file created earlier in **Exercise 4**. It is assumed that the `resume2.html` file resides in the same folder as the `photo.html` file (the Desktop folder, for example).

To link to another page in the same folder or path:

1. Use **File | Open** to open the `photo.html` file created earlier in **Exercise 4**.
2. Use the Window menu to select `resume2.html` to make it the active document.
3. Highlight and select the words "Thomas B. Seeker" at the top of the resume document.
4. Choose **Insert | Hyperlink**. The Create Hyperlink dialog box appears.
5. Choose the **Open Pages** tab, select "Photo of Thomas B. Seeker" (see Figure 17), then choose **OK**. You may see a warning that this is a local page and it may not be available after it is posted to the Web. In reality, these pages are on the Web server. Choose **Yes**. The hyperlinked text is now underlined.
6. Save the changes. When the source code is viewed with **View | HTML...**, `<a href="photo.html"> </a>` encloses the "Thomas B. Seeker" text (see Figure 18).
7. Switch back to the browser window and update the document as it appears in the browser.

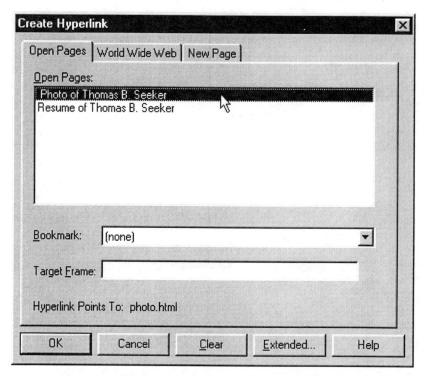

Figure 17. In the **Create Hyperlink** box, select "Photo of Thomas B. Seeker."

8. Test the link. If the tags are entered correctly, "Thomas B. Seeker" indicates it is a hypertext link. When this link is chosen, the browser looks for and displays photo.html as a Web page.

Exercise 8-3: URL links

Linking to another Web site follows the same procedure as linking to another location within an existing Web site, except that it is necessary to provide the entire URL of the destination site. Because URLs must be entered exactly (no typos and same case), you may find it easier to copy and paste a URL rather than to type it.

To create a link to another Web site:

1. Highlight and select the words, "Science Applications International Corporation (SAIC)," in the "Professional Experience" section of the resume2.html file.
2. Choose **Insert | Hyperlink....** The **Create Hyperlink** dialog box appears.
3. Choose the **World Wide Web** tab.
4. Select http: from the **Hyperlink Type** drop-down list.
5. Enter http://www.saic.alaska.net in the **URL** text box (see Figure 19).
6. Choose **OK**.
7. Save the changes. When viewed in the **View | HTML...** window, <a href="http://www.saic.alaska.net" name="Accomplishments"> </a> encloses the "Science Applications International Corporation (SAIC)" text.

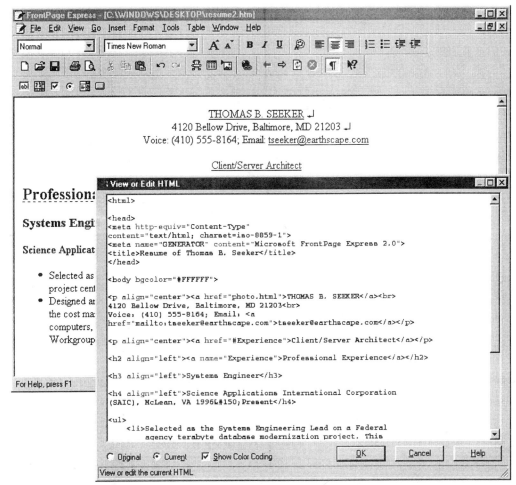

Figure 18. FrontPage Express and the **View or Edit HTML** window showing the results of adding the hyperlink to the "Thomas B. Seeker" text.

8. Switch back to the browser window and update the document.
9. Test the link. If the tags are correct, "Science Applications International Corporation (SAIC)" will indicate it is a hypertext link. When this link is chosen, the browser will look for and display `http://www.saic.alaska.net`, the Web page for the Science Applications International Corporation (SAIC).

Exercise 9: Inserting images

1. Open the `photo.html` file created earlier in **Exercise 4**.
2. Choose **View | HTML....**
3. Insert the following element tag between the `<BODY>` `</BODY>` tag pair combination. Enclose the name of the image file within quotation marks. To insert your photo into your page, you would type:

```
<BODY> <IMG SRC="photo.jpg"> </BODY>
```

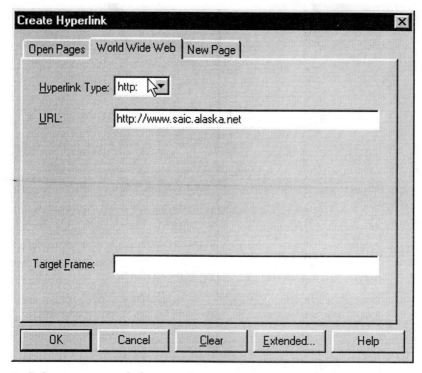

Figure 19. Select `http:` and then enter `http://www.saic.alaska.net` as the link's URL.

`<IMG SRC=>` instructs the browser to load the specified image, located in the same folder as the current Web page.

4. Save the changes. The `photo.jpg` image should appear in the document. If the image does not appear, ensure that the `photo.html` and `photo.jpg` files are located in the same folder, and the filename in the tag is typed *exactly* the same way you initially saved it.

5. Images can also be inserted by using **Insert | Image...**. However, the dialog box requires the full path name (such as `c:\windows\desktop\photo.jpg` or the complete URL). Please note, that once the `photo.html` file is posted to the Web, you will not want to have it pointing to the image on your hard drive because no one will be able to access the file. Therefore, to eliminate the need for listing full path names for local images, manually insert the `<IMG SRC=>` code.

Exercise 10: Inserting a WebBot

WebBots are tools included with FrontPage Express that automate common tasks encountered when creating Web pages. With these tools, maintaining your Web site is a snap. FrontPage Express provides three WebBots—**Include**, **Search**, and **Timestamp**. Many more WebBots are available in the fully-functional version of FrontPage 98.

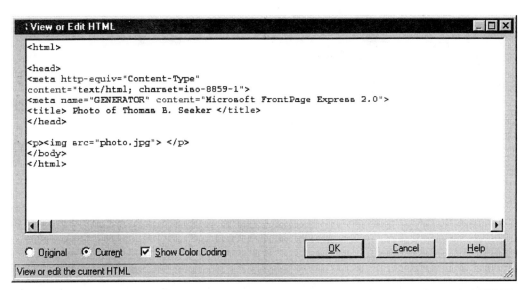

Figure 20. Enter the `<IMG SRC=>` tag information after selecting **View | HTML...** to ensure that you can specify the file locally (rather than using a full path name).

The Timestamp WebBot is quite useful. Timestamp marks the Web page with the last time you modified the page. This allows visitors to your Web resume to see how current it is. Each time your Web resume is updated, save it, then post the latest version to the Web. The Timestamp Bot automatically reflects the date you made the changes.

WebBots only work on Web sites that support FrontPage extensions. If you are not sure whether your Web site supports FrontPage extensions, ask your Internet service provider.

Avoid posting the timestamp if your Web resume will not be updated on a regular basis. Pages announcing that it was updated a year ago appear stale even before a visitor reads the content.

To add the Timestamp WebBot to the Web resume:

1. Open the `resume.html` file that you created earlier in **Exercise 1** in Front-Page Express. Place the cursor at the bottom of the page and enter the following text:

   `Last updated on .`

2. Place the cursor to the left of the period (that is, between "on" and "."), then choose **Insert | WebBot Component...**.
3. Select "Timestamp," then choose **OK** (see Figure 22).
4. Select "Date this page was last automatically updated," then the "date format" selection from the **Date Format** drop-down list, then choose **OK** (see Figure 21).
5. The current date appears. The date field will automatically update whenever you edit and save the page.

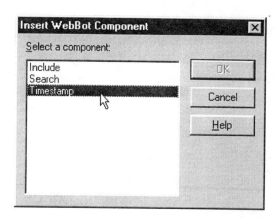

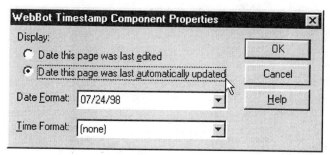

Figure 21. After selecting the Timestamp WebBot and choosing **OK**, specify the date format.

Converting a print resume using Microsoft Word

Word 97 and 98 can automatically generate HTML files much like FrontPage Express. It's as easy as typing what you want to see on the Web page and then saving it as an HTML file (.htm or .html) rather than a standard Word file.

Word 97 and 98 allow you to open WordPerfect documents, as well as rich-text format files, among others. Working with a familiar word processor, you can use the standard formatting features you are accustomed to using—bold, italic, underline, center, numbered lists, bulleted lists, and tables. Word 97 and 98 automatically convert these formats into their HTML counterparts. Using these applications, you can also insert images, bookmarks, and hyperlinks by way of the **Insert** menu.

When you convert Word documents to HTML, graphics and other components are also converted and saved to their Internet counterparts. Word converts clip art, stored in Windows MetaFile (.wmf) format, into a Web-standard .gif file.

HTML layout features in Word 97 and Word 98

The process of creating an online resume is simple—save your Word 97 or 98 resume in HTML format. Saving to HTML, however, does have some limitations. HTML supports fewer layout features, compared to those supported by popular word-processing programs.

HTML supports some common word processing and page layout formatting features. However, simple formatting we take for granted, such as tabs and page numbering, are not supported. You can get around many of these limitations by using features available in HTML to create the same effect.

Exercise 11: Converting an existing Microsoft Word file to HTML

This exercise illustrates how to open and convert an existing Microsoft Word file to HTML. It also illustrates how to view the code once converted.

Exercise 11-1: Open an existing file in Microsoft Word

Word automatically adds all of the required HTML tags—<HTML> </HTML>, <HEAD> </HEAD>, <TITLE> </TITLE>, and <BODY> </BODY>. It also adds standard formatting tags—<P> </P>, <B> </B>, <UL> </UL>, <LI>, and more—based on the formatting of the original "print" document. Word adds <META> tags between the <HEAD> </HEAD> tags. These tags include additional information about the software that created the page.

To convert a Word file to HTML:

1. Choose **File | Open**, select a file you previously created (open a copy of your own resume, resume.doc), then choose **Open**.
2. Choose **File | Save**.
3. Save the file to HTML format, giving it the filename resume3.html

   - **Word 97 or Word 98:** Choose **File | Save as HTML....** The **File name:** text box defaults to the .htm file extension and the **Save as type:** drop-down list automatically defaults to "HTML Document" (*.htm, *.html, *.htx). As shown in Figure 22, specify which of the three file extensions to use, then choose **Save**. Answer **Yes** or **No**, as appropriate, if asked whether you want to check the Internet for a new version of Web page authoring tools.
   - **Word 6.0a (or higher) or Word 95 with Internet Assistant add-on:** Choose **File | Save as....** Choose "HTML Document" (*.htm) from the **Save as type** drop-down list.

4. Open your Web-ready resume with Microsoft Internet Explorer, Netscape Communicator, or another Web browser. Depending upon which browser you are using, font size and margins may adjust themselves.
5. If it looks great and does not require any changes, you are ready to publish it to the Web. The most common starting is your ISP. Depending on the type of account you have, ask them for the procedures to transfer your HTML files onto their Web server. If it does not look that good, fine-tune the formatting in a text-based HTML editor (such as Notepad or SimpleText) or graphical HTML editor, such as FrontPage Express.

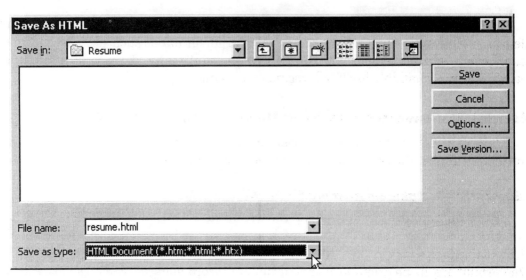

Figure 22. Save a Word document to HTML format.

Congratulations—you have now created an HTML version of your resume! See, it wasn't that hard! Now its time to fiddle with the code and make it work more efficiently. **Exercise 11-2** will describe how to view the HTML source code while still in Microsoft Word. **Exercises 12** through **16** illustrate various tasks for fine-tuning the code.

Exercise 11-2: View the HTML source code

The **HTML Source** command is only visible in the **View** menu when working with HTML documents. The screen changes the view to the HTML source code and allows direct editing of HTML. This is a very important function, because there may be times when you will need to remove or modify an HTML tag that cannot be directly manipulated in Word. This view also serves as a good learning tool—after converting your resume to HTML, you can look at the resulting source code and see how your Web page really works.

To view the HTML source code:

1. Choose **View | HTML Source** (see Figure 23).
2. Scroll through the document and check out your code.
3. Return to original view.

   - **Microsoft Word 97 or Word 98:** Choose **View | Exit HTML Source.**
   - **Word 6.0a (or higher) or Word 95 with Internet Assistant add-on:** Choose **View | Return To Edit Mode.**

In most cases, formatting created in the original Word document (such as tables, bullets, and bold type) is completely retained in the newly created HTML document. If it isn't retained, you will have to add it manually. Use **Exercises 12** through **16** to fine-tune the formatting of your Web resume.

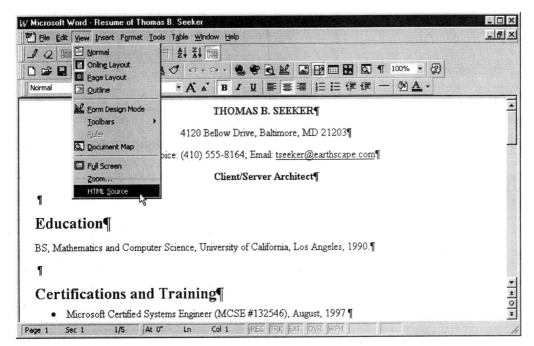

Figure 23. Select **View | HTML Source** to view HTML code in Word.

Exercise 12: Using a table to align text

Because HTML does not yet support tabs, the tabs are viewed only as spaces. Take a look at how text aligns in your document. If you have text aligned with tabs, it is necessary to adjust the formatting so that it does not depend on tabs. Or, try using a table.

Placing text in a table creates the illusion of tab-aligned text, as well as the illusion of margins and columns. In an HTML table, as in a Word table, you can merge cells to align text, and apply different formatting attributes to the text in each cell.

There are several advantages to placing text in a table:

- You can give your Web page a left-side margin for a little of that valuable white space.
- You can control how far to the right your text flows in the Web browser window.
- You can create bulleted text using .gif bullet graphics, placing the graphic in one column and the text in the next column.
- Not all browsers support tables. Browsers that do not support tables may jumble the display of your Web page.
- Some browsers recognize empty columns or rows, providing the capability of creating the illusion of additional white space. Browsers that do not recognize empty columns or rows will simply ignore them.

- If the <FONT> </FONT> tag pair is used within the body of a table, it must be repeated for all table cells (<TD> </TD> tag pairs) within that table. Word does this for you automatically. However, if you are hand coding, you must enter the redundant codes yourself.

Exercise 12-1: Use Word to insert and format a table

Tables play an important role in formatting and arranging text. In Microsoft Word, a table is a grid of rows and columns containing boxes called "cells."

To insert a table using Word:

1. Choose **Table | Insert Table....**
2. Enter the number of columns and rows, then choose **OK**. Word inserts a table similar to the following. For example, if you specify three columns and four rows, the following table is inserted. Tables inserted with Word 97 and 98 automatically apply a thin border to the outline of each cell. Tables inserted with Word 6.0a and 95 are created without a border. The table created with Word 97 or 98 resembles the following. You can choose to keep the cell borders or remove them.

3. Choose **File | Save.**

To remove the cell borders:

1. Select the table. Position the cursor to the left of the table. Press the left mouse button, move the mouse downward to highlight the entire table, then release the mouse button.
2. Choose **Format | Borders and Shading....**
3. Choose **Border | None**, then choose **OK**. When you remove the borders from the table, dotted gridlines appear, indicating the location of the table cells. These gridlines do not appear in the Web browser view, nor do they appear when the table is printed. You can leave the cell formatting as is, or apply other formatting changes (such as changing the cell height and width or merging cells).
4. Choose **File | Save.**

To adjust cell height and width:

1. Select some portion of the table or simply place the cursor in one of the table cells.
2. Choose **Table | Cell Height and Width....**

3. Specify the desired width for columns and height for rows, then choose **OK**.
4. Choose **File | Save**.

To merge cells:

1. Position the cursor in the first cell to merge.
2. Press SHIFT, then select the next cell to merge, and so forth. The selected cells should now appear highlighted.
3. Choose **Table | Merge Cells**.
4. Choose **File | Save**.

Exercise 12-2: General use of tables

To insert and format tables, you can use Word, a graphical HTML editor (such as FrontPage Express), or other word processor application that supports tables to create the same effect.

For example, the following is a portion of the sample Web resume text:

Professional Experience

Science Applications International Corporation (SAIC), McLean, VA
1996-Present

Systems Engineer

- Selected as Systems Engineering Lead on a federal agency terabyte database modernization project. This project centered on migrating from mainframe to client/server technology.
- Designed and managed the development of an enterprise-level client/server automated auditing application for the cost management division of a major long-distance telephone service provider. Migrated from mainframe computers, db2, and FOCUS to workgroup-oriented, client/server arch-itecture involving Windows for Workgroups, Windows NT Server, Microsoft SQL Server, Oracle7, and UNIX.
- Conducted extensive trade studies of a large number of vendors that offered leading-edge technologies; these studies identified proven (low-risk) implementations of symmetric multiprocessing computers (SMP) and Relational Database Management Systems (RDBMS) that met stringent performance and availability criteria.

To use a table to align text:

1. Determine how many columns and rows needed for the previously referenced "Professional Experience" text block. For this example, specify three columns and four rows.
2. Create the table, merging cells as necessary to accommodate alignment.
3. Enter the text into the appropriate cells.

Professional Experience	
Science Applications International Corporation (SAIC), McLean, VA	*1996-Present*
Systems Engineer	
	Selected as Systems Engineering Lead on a Federal agency terabyte database modernization project. This project centered on migrating from mainframe to client/server technology.
	Designed and managed the development of an enterprise-level client/server automated auditing application for the cost management division of a major long-distance telephone service provider. Migrated from mainframe computers, db2, and FOCUS to workgroup oriented, client/server architecture involving Windows for Workgroups, Windows NT Server, Microsoft SQL Server, Oracle7, and UNIX.
	Conducted extensive trade studies of a large number of vendors that offered leading-edge technologies; these studies identified proven (low-risk) implementations of symmetric multiprocessing computers (SMP) and Relational Database Management Systems (RDBMS) that met stringent performance and availability criteria.

Figure 24. Data converted into table form in Word.

4. Specify the horizontal alignment for each cell.
5. Choose **File | Save**. Figure 24 shows a completed table, ready for posting on the Internet.

Exercise 13: Watching your fonts

A font is a design of text characters (letters, punctuation, and numbers). Helvetica, Times, Arial, and Geneva are all examples of font names. Font size, which is measured in points, is the size of the characters. A point is a standard measurement in the publishing industry. There are 72 points in an inch.

Although fonts can be specified in HTML documents, you cannot be sure they'll be seen the same way on the Web. To help ensure that your Web resume always looks its best, use common fonts installed on most computers. Don't try anything too exotic—chances are they won't work on your potential employer's computer. Arial and Times New Roman are the two most frequently used Web browser default fonts—stick with them.

Exercise 13-1: Specify a font

You can specify fonts by:

- Using the **Font** and **Font Size** drop-down lists in the Word toolbar.
- Using the **Format | Font...** command.
- Manually inserting the HTML code when using **View | HTML Source**.

The first two techniques are useful when you only want to specify one font or when you do not know the name of the font you want to use. The latter technique is useful if you know exactly which font you want, as well as for specifying a hierarchy of default fonts, as described in **Exercise 13-2**.

To specify a font using the Font and Font Size drop-down lists:

1. Open the `resume.html` file.
2. Select the "Thomas B. Seeker" text.
3. Choose the down arrow button of the **Font** drop-down list to display the list of fonts installed on your computer. The font names in your list may differ from those shown in Figure 25.
4. Scroll through the list, then select the font you want to use. The selected text now appears in the selected font.
5. Choose the **Increase Font Size** button to enlarge the text (see Figure 25).
6. The HTML code for the "Thomas B. Seeker" text may now resemble the following:

   ```
   <B> <FONT FACE="TIMES NEW ROMAN" SIZE=5> <P> THOMAS B. SEEKER
   <BR> </B> </FONT>
   ```

7. Return to original view.

   - **Microsoft Word 97 or Word 98:** Choose **View | Exit HTML Source**.
   - **Word 6.0a (or higher) or Word 95 with Internet Assistant add-on:** Choose **View | Return To Edit Mode**.

If no FACE attribute is specified, the document is probably using the default font set by your Word processor.

Font size is measured differently in the HTML source code. Although you may have specified 12 or 24, you may see numbers such as 3 or 5. The SIZE attribute values range from 1 (tiny) to 7 (fairly big), with 3 being the default. The font size depends upon the resolution of individual computer screens and browser preference settings. Specifying a font size helps control how the font appears to others; not specifying a font causes the text to use defaults set by other viewers' Web browsers.

It is not necessary to use the SIZE attribute with heading tags. Heading tag pairs automatically create a hierarchy of sizes that are dependent on the browser's preference settings. Although it is not necessary, Word may also use the FONT SIZE attribute in tandem with the heading tags.

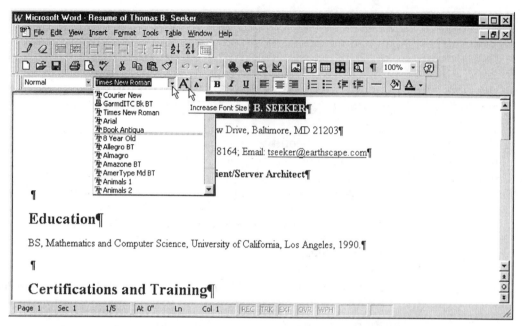

Figure 25. Select the "Thomas B. Seeker" text on the document, the font from the drop-down font list, then use the **Increase Font Size** button to enlarge it.

Exercise 13-2: Specify a hierarchy of default fonts

In HTML, you can specify a hierarchy of fonts for text so that if the first font is not available to the Web browser, the second is used, and so forth. For instance, if you want a sans serif font to give contrast to your headings, specify "Helvetica, Arial, Geneva." The browser then searches for those fonts in that order. The odds are that one will be found, as Helvetica is installed with the Windows, UNIX, and the Macintosh operating systems; Arial with Windows; and Geneva with the Macintosh. If none of the specified fonts is found, the browser uses the default font (as defined in the browser preference settings).

To see what fonts are specified in your Web resume:

1. Open the `resume.html` file.
2. Choose **View | HTML Source**.
3. Scroll through the HTML code. Look for the FACE attribute, which is always part of the `<FONT> </FONT>` tag pair. For example:

   `<FONT FACE="ARIAL"> Systems Engineer </FONT>`

4. If the `FACE` attribute is not specified for some of your text, that text will use the browser's default font. If it is there and you want the text to display in the browser's default font, remove the `FACE` attribute and variable.
5. If you want to specify a hierarchy of fonts rather than a single font, replace the `FACE` variable text with a string of variables, listing the fonts you want browsers to use. For example:

```
<FONT FACE="ARIAL, GENEVA, HELVETICA"> Systems Engineer </FONT>
```

6. Return to original view.

- **Microsoft Word 97 or Word 98:** Choose **View | Exit HTML Source**.
- **Word 6.0a (or higher) or Word 95 with Internet Assistant add-on:** Choose **View | Return To Edit Mode**.

Exercise 13-3: Applying color text

Although HTML does not convert highlighted text to anything other than just text, it does convert color applied to text as colored text. Highlighted text in Word creates a boxy effect, similar to the effect of using a highlighter pen. Users can "highlight" text in HTML simply by applying a `<FONT COLOR=""> </FONT>` to text.

To apply color to text:

1. Open the `resume.html` file.
2. Select the "Systems Engineer" text.
3. Choose the **Color** drop-down arrow, then select a color from the flyout list (see Figure 26).
4. Choose **File | Save**.
5. Choose **View | HTML Source**. Note the addition of the COLOR attribute. In **Exercise 13-1**, the Systems Engineer HTML code sample provided appeared as follows:

   ```
   <FONT FACE="ARIAL"> Systems Engineer </FONT>
   ```

   By applying a color to the text, the `<FONT>` tag now includes a COLOR attribute and variable, similar to the following:

   ```
   <FONT FACE="ARIAL" COLOR="#0000ff"> Systems Engineer </FONT>
   ```

   The strange looking numbers #0000ff are code representations for RGB color (Red Green Blue). These codes translate into actual color. For example, `<FONT COLOR="0000ff">` is the same as entering `<FONT COLOR="BLUE">`. If you were to manually code HTML, you could simply specify the color name. Otherwise, the application defaults by using the numbers when you select a color from a drop-down menu in Word.

6. Return to original view.

- **Microsoft Word 97 or 98:** Choose **View | Exit HTML Source**.
- **Word 6.0a (or higher) or 95 with Internet Assistant add-on:** Choose **View | Return To Edit Mode**.

Exercise 14: Adding a hyperlink

Links are easy to create and keep track of in Microsoft Word. This exercise describes how to create and edit an e-mail hyperlink. Creation of other types of hyperlinks was discussed previously in **Exercises 4 and 8** of this chapter.

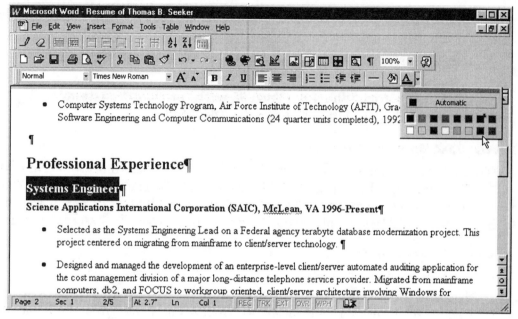

Figure 26. Select text to be formatted, then select a color from the flyout list.

Exercise 14-1: Create an e-mail hyperlink

For your e-mail address, create a MAILTO hyperlink to make it easy for potential employers to contact you. Most browsers will open an e-mail message window addressed to you when visitors choose this link on the Web. You might also want to include this link at the end of your page. Potential employers can then contact you after reading your resume, without having to go back to the top of the page.

Word 97 and 98 provide the ability to insert e-mail and other hyperlinks into your document without having to write any HTML code.

To place an e-mail hyperlink into your resume:

1. Open the resume.html file, then scroll to the end of the file.
2. Choose **Insert | Hyperlink...**. Choose **Yes** if prompted to save the file. The **Insert Hyperlink** dialog box appears (see Figure 27).
3. Enter MAILTO:, followed by the e-mail address to which you where to receive e-mail messages. For example, in the **Link to file or URL** text box, enter an e-mail address like the following:

   MAILTO:tseeker@earthscape.com

4. Choose **OK** to apply the e-mail hyperlink.

Exercise 14-2: Edit an e-mail hyperlink

Word 97 and Word 98 make it easy to edit links. You will need to know this process so you can keep your hyperlinks up-to-date, such as when the URL of one of the pages to which you are linking changes.

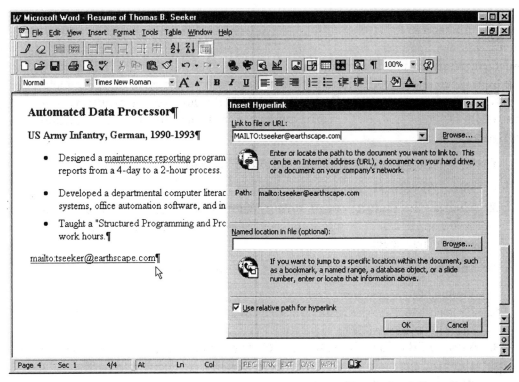

Figure 27. Insert Hyperlink dialog box and the effect of adding the MAILTO hyperlink to the text.

To edit existing links:

1. Open the `resume.html` file.
2. Place the mouse cursor on the link to be modified, then press the secondary mouse button (typically a right-click).
3. Choose **Hyperlink | Edit Hyperlink...**.
4. Modify the text of the link (for example, an e-mail address or URL).
5. Choose **OK** to apply the new hyperlink.

Exercise 15: Adding background color

In **Exercise 5-3**, you learned how to apply a background image to your Web resume. In this exercise, you will learn how to apply a background color or background image to your Web resume. Both provide a "backdrop" to the document and force the browser to use your selected "background," rather than the browser's default background color, such as gray. If in doubt as to how the background color or image will look online, choose **View | Online Layout**. Keep in mind that you can use either background colors or patterns—but not both.

The tabs that appear in the **Fill Effects** dialog box may vary, depending on which items you selected or deselected when you installed Microsoft Word. When choosing background colors for your Web resume, avoid overly bright or dark colors, as this makes for difficult reading. Avoid bright, solid-colored backgrounds (such as reds, yellows, oranges, and greens). These can quickly become tiring to the eyes. Also, remember that background colors do not show up when your Web resume is printed. This is especially important if you decide to use reverse text (such as white text on a dark background). Because background colors do not print, reversed text is unreadable when printed to white paper. Sometimes black or a gradation of gray are your best bets.

To add background color to your Web resume:

1. Open the `resume.html` file.
2. Choose the **Background** button, then select a color from the flyout menu (see Figure 28). If you cannot read the text in contrast to the selected color, try another color.

To select a background image for your Web resume:

1. Open the `resume.html` file.
2. Choose the **Background** button, then choose **Fill Effects...** from the flyout menu (see Figure 29).
3. Select a fill effect, then choose **OK**. The fill now appears in the background of the document. If you cannot read the text in contrast to the selected fill, repeat steps 2 and 3.

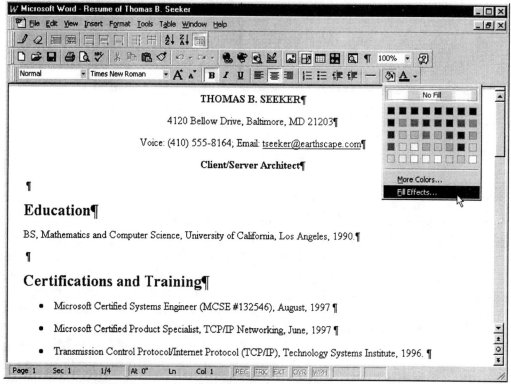

Figure 28. Select a background color from the flyout menu.

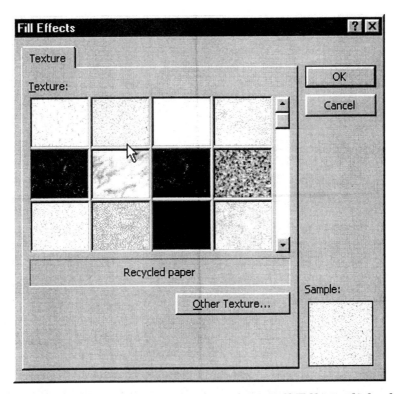

Figure 29. Select a background fill the from **Fill Effects** dialog box.

- **Word 97 or Word 98:** Image1.gif, Image2.gif, and so forth.
- **Word 6.0a (or higher) or Word 95 with Internet Assistant add-on:** Img0001.gif, Img0002.gif, and so forth.

Keep the document and image files in the same folder. Additionally, do not rename the image files, because you will break the link in your HTML file that points to them.

To add an image to your Web resume:

1. Open the resume.html file.
2. Choose **Insert | Picture**, then choose **Clip Art...** or **From File...**.
3. Locate the image, changing folders and paths as necessary, then choose **Insert**. The image now appears in the file.

Chapter 10

Search Engine-savvy Web Resumes

The linked nature of the Web makes Web resumes effective job networking tools—your personal Web pages become your portfolio, resume, and business card all rolled into one. Unlike Web-based resume databases that attract the attention of employers and recruiters by promoting their large databases, Web resumes must attract the attention of interested employers and recruiters on their own. Your Web resume must stand out in a sea of more than 300 million other Web pages and survive the scarcest commodity of all: the reader's attention span.

People usually find your Web resume by linking to it from some other source. Most people find other sites by using search engines. The key is designing your Web resume to get the attention necessary for them to link to you in the first place. An obvious starting point for getting employers to visit your Web resume is to register its URL with popular search engines.

Unfortunately, because of the Web's size and design, your resume can get lost very easily. Most search engines use their own proprietary searching strategies independently of others; there are no standards in search and retrieval methods. Also, there is no single comprehensive index or systematic organization to the Web. Search engines help to minimize some of this randomness when you register the URL. Because search engine databases differ so much, searches on different engines naturally produce different results. In order to tame this jungle of information to meet your job search needs, you should do two things:

1. Learn about search engines.
2. Think like a recruiter when designing your Web resume.

Many job-seekers are concerned with getting the highest number of "hits" possible at their Web resume, but that is like mass-mailing your paper resume to hundreds of employers. Both techniques are useless if they don't produce what a resume is intended to provide: job interviews.

Your understanding of these two processes will affect your decisions on which search engine you select to submit your Web resume's URL, and what design strategies you choose to make your Web resume stand out during a search.

The effective use of search engines is crucial to your online job hunt. Knowing what search engines are popular enables you to find job information easily. The two main Internet search engine tools available are *subject directory* and *keyword* searches.

Subject directories

A subject directory search engine is much like the "yellow pages" section in a phone book. Subject directories are hierarchically organized indexes of subject categories that allow you to browse through lists of Web sites by subject. A subject directory's database is organized by subject matter. A subject directory will display general subject headings and move down to increasingly more specific subheadings.

Yahoo! (http://www.yahoo.com) and Magellan (http://magellan.excite.com) are two subject directories. Both take your keywords and return a list of categories and Web sites.

Subject directories tend to be smaller than keyword indexes, which means that result lists tend to be smaller as well. However, one advantage of subject directories is that because a directory like Yahoo! is prescreened by human reviewers, reducing the number of irrelevant sites.

Keyword indexes

Keyword indexes often lack the hierarchical structure of directories, relying much more on computing horsepower to retrieve entire Web pages into their database, then analyze the retrieved documents with indexing software.

Most search engines access databases by using keywords, which are common descriptor terms for information you seek. A search engine reasons to a specific query with a list of matching references or "hits." Using a search engine is sometimes called doing a "keyword search."

Spiders are used by search engines to "crawl" around the Net and gather information. They can index entire Web sites by examining a Web page, record the words that appear on it, and then categorize it based on those words. With criteria established by the user and/or the search engine, the index retrieves Web pages from its database that match the keywords entered by the searcher.

Although a subject directory is more likely to return a list of categories with links only to a Web site's home page, a keyword index typically indexes every page of a given Web site. AltaVista is an example of a keyword index that takes your keywords and returns a list of Web pages. Alta Vista's spider, called "Scooter," collects and indexes every word found on every Web document. Search results indicate whether one or more of the search terms appears within a Web page. When a spider visits your resume's URL, it will record the full text of its page.

Keyword indexes are best used to find specific pieces of information, like a well-known Web page, rather than a general subject or topic. However, many of the popular keyword indexes are adding a directory-based format to their search engine Web site interface.

Your registration tags

Exactly what kind of information a spider gathers from a Web page depends upon the specific indexing characteristics of the search engine.

Once a search engine's spider is at a site, it reports back to the search engines and indexing begins. When you search for the word "resume," the search engine submits that term to the index. The index then finds the word and displays a list of pages containing it.

Because search engines index only HTML or text formats, some things won't be indexed:

- Registration or password-based access.
- Heavy use of images and image maps.
- Specialized formats like PostScript and Acrobat files.
- Text within framesets.
- Multimedia files.
- Large (more than 4 MB or more than 2,000 pages of text) text files.
- Dynamic content that is frequently and automatically updated.

Indexing varies among the search engines. Some engines index the entire contents of the page. These are called full-text indexes because they index every word found on every Web page in their databases.

Other engines index only specific parts, such as the `<TITLE>` tag. If you recall, in Chapter 9 you learned how to use a `<TITLE>` tag.

The `<TITLE>` tag is what a browser will display in its title bar. It isn't just the first line of HTML that shows up on your page. Search engines such as Alta Vista will display the text located between the `<TITLE>` tags when your Web page is listed in a search. By making your `<TITLE>` descriptive, you also make it helpful when people bookmark your site. If a more descriptive name appears in a person's hotlist, it will be easier to find your site at a later date. Something cryptic or vague will eventually find its way to an employer's "recycling bin."

Search engines also look at keywords embedded in `<META>` tags located at the top of the page to categorize your Web site's content. As you recall from Chapter 9, `<META>` tags provide information about the page itself—including its subject, author, content, and keywords—that search engines and software agents use to index and retrieve documents.

The HTML Writer's Guild (http://www.hwg.org) recommends that before you start adding `<META>` tags to your Web pages, to be aware that not all search engines use the tags, and those that do don't all use them the same way. There's no specification for exactly how to implement these features. Your best guidance is to refer to the submission guidelines provided at the search engine Web site where you want to submit your Web resume's URL.

The standard tags that search engines use are the DESCRIPTION and KEYWORDS <META> tags. The syntax is:

```
<META> NAME="description" CONTENT="your site description here">
<META> NAME="keywords" CONTENT="keywords for your site here">
```

The keyword <META> tag is used by most of the largest search engines to catalog the Web site. This tag helps to improve the cataloging of the page in several of the major search engines, including Alta Vista, Lycos, Infoseek, HotBot, Open Text, Northern Light and WebCrawler.

Many search engines also use the information in the description <META> tag to create the summary for the page.

There are several ways you can control how a search engine will index your site to ensure your potential readers can find your Web resume. For example, this file consists of ASCII text punctuated with paired tags enclosed in angle brackets—one turns on a formatting command. The basic syntax is as follows:

```
<HTML>
<HEAD>
<TITLE> Thomas B. Seeker's Resume </TITLE>
<META NAME="Description" content="My Resume">
<META NAME="Keywords" content="Systems Analyst, Resume, Windows 95,
Project Manager, Programmer">
<BODY>
[Body of Resume]
</BODY>
</HEAD>
```

Because most keyword indexes do not perform any content analysis, keyword indexes assign relevance scores to the pages in the search results. In general, the highest scores go to pages that include descriptive search terms in the <TITLE> tag, keywords and phrases in the <META> tags, and overall content on the page.

When a spider visits your Web resume, it will go first to the <TITLE> tag. The <TITLE> tag is what a browser will display in its title bar. For example, instead of using "<TITLE> Tom's Resume </TITLE>" as the title of your resume, "<TITLE> Client/Server Architect Resume for Thomas B. Seeker </TITLE>" is more descriptive. It places greater emphasis on "Systems Analyst" when calculating keywords.

The indexing characteristics of AltaVista, Infoseek, and WebCrawler make wide use of <TITLE> tags. In fact, an AltaVista search for "systems analyst resumes" revealed that the most relevant resume returned out of 200,000 contained a simple five-word <TITLE> tag.

Because search engines only index a limited amount of text for each item, it's best to keep to around 150 characters for descriptions and 750 for keyword <META>

tags. Although <META> tags are not visible to someone who looks at the site (unless they look through your source code), they are critical in determining what search terms will lead someone to your Web resume. Refer to Appendix D for the indexing characteristics of the more popular search engines.

A Web resume success story

Carol Calhoun, a senior employee benefits attorney, is an example of what is possible with a carefully designed and strategically placed Web resume. Creating her Web resume became a source of fun, as well as an excellent job-hunting tool. Her savvy resume networking techniques got her several inquiries within one week of posting her Web resume, and three offers shortly thereafter. She ended up accepting one of them, as a shareholder in a nationwide law firm.

Employers whom she had never contacted called her and asked her to interview with them. These were all potential employers she might never have come into contact with otherwise.

This response did wonders for her morale. She discovered her skills were in demand and could concentrate on pursuing only those opportunities where she knew she would be a good fit.

Carol found that her Web resume had been far and away her most successful job-hunting technique—much more effective than search firms who used more traditional ways of finding jobs in her field. Let's take a look at some of the strategies Carol used to get those interviews

Initial design considerations

Carol had two goals in mind when she created her Web resume:

1. To appeal to other attorneys who did not necessarily have the latest in computer systems and Web browsers.
2. To use her Web resume as a client-development tool after she completed her job search. These two goals were the basis for designing her Web resume with her target audience in mind, and choosing the tools and resources she would need.

As you can see in Figure 1, Carol's Web resume makes a host of information available and accessible. Everything from copies of recent speeches and articles to her academic accomplishments can be accessed from hyperlinks, while avoiding overwhelming the reader by presenting a one-screen resume.

From a page layout standpoint, Carol debated on whether to list her substantive experience first (running the risk that potential employers would not browse far enough down to figure out how to contact her) or providing her contact information first (which meant that the first screen might show none of the information that would encourage interested potential employers to read further).

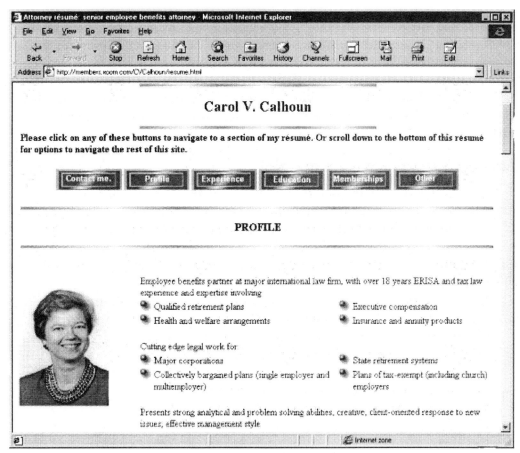

Figure 1. Carol Calhoun on the Web

On looking at some of the models on my eResumes & Resources Web site (http://www.eresumes.com). (Allow me to plug *my* Web site for a moment. eResumes.com provides a gallery of Web resumes, writing tips, and other pieces of "great to know" information. There are also countless links to other resources in order to give your e-resume the competitive edge it needs.) After browsing through some examples, she chose to use a navigation bar at the top of her Web resume, with links to important information. This let her have contact information as the very first item on the navigation bar (so that employers will realize that they can contact her if they like what they see). Because the navigation bar took up only one line of precious screen space, she placed all of the important information within the first screen. She also added contact information at the bottom of the Web resume.

From a technical standpoint, Carol designed her Web resume so that it could be read by early versions of the Netscape Navigator or Microsoft Internet Explorer browsers. Carol also designed her Web resume to accommodate the average 15-inch computer monitor. This minimized chances that a recruiter would have to scroll left and right. More importantly, this also minimized the chance that when the pages were printed, text might be cut off at the margins.

Carol also included a convenient hyperlink that provided recruiters with the option of printing a text-only version of her resume. This is especially useful if some of the needed information on the Web resume is contained as a link to separate pages. She found that by doing this, she could enable someone to print the text-only version, and have it look like a traditionally printed resume. In one instance, a search firm even saved her resume, modified it using a word processing program, and sent it out to interested clients.

Including a professional photograph

There is debate on whether to include a photo with any kind of resume, as it might be grounds for discrimination during the screening and hiring process. Carol chose to include a photograph of herself, which appears in the first viewing screen of her resume. Carol felt that adding a photo of herself helped establish a sense of approachability to otherwise nervous recruiters who might feel uncomfortable about cold-calling someone from a Web resume.

The photograph also served as a screening tool on her behalf. She at least knew that when she received those phone calls, there was a greater chance of starting off on the right foot prior to the interview. Including a professional photo on a Web resume takes advantage of the uniqueness of the Web—people must seek you out. When prospective employers find you and call you, you have passed that first hurdle in getting an interview: You already have their interest.

Finding suitable Web space

Many sites on the Web offer no-cost space on their servers for ordinary people and businesses, as well as students, actors, advocates of diversity or free speech, artists, programmers, and other special-interest groups. Nonprofit and religious organizations also can find a "free" home. The advantage is that everything is online. All you need is Internet access. On the negative side, you will not always be able to retain full control over content, the sites can be slow, and sometimes there are waiting lists for space. If a site offering free space requires a credit card number, or asks you to buy an account on its system, back off. You are better off paying for service.

GeoCities (http://www.geocities.com) is a very popular site that offers free home pages, a utility that helps users create home pages, and an FTP utility for uploading your own custom pages. Browse the different neighborhoods organized by various themes to see how you might fit in and what vacancies are available. Once your application is approved, you can also obtain no-cost e-mail services.

Free Web space listings can be found in Yahoo! (http://www.yahoo.com) by searching on the keywords, "free Web space". Another resource is the Free WebSpace Review (http://206.161.225.56/~maxlee/FWPReview), where you can find up-to-date comparison tables with links to no-cost Web space provider services. Personal and special-interest areas (business, gaming, politics, religion, etc.) are also categorized. They are further subcategorized by country, language, and disk space—2 MB and under, 3 to 9 MB, and 10 MB and over. As of this writing, there are more than 124 no-cost Web space providers indexed for personal use, from more than 21 countries and languages.

Many academic institutions and ISPs allow their members to retain free Web pages. Consult your ISP or institute administrator for more details.

Carol took advantage of one of the numerous free Web page builders. This gave her the freedom and flexibility to experiment, without spending a lot of money in the process. After looking at many free services, she chose Xoom. Xoom did not distinguish between commercial or personal use (GeoCities charged a fee for commercial use—a fine line for a Web resume that would also serve as a client development tool later on). Xoom also offered quite a bit of free Web space to work with at 11 MB for both personal and commercial use.

Xoom did not require Carol place distracting banner ads on her pages in exchange for the free space, like GeoCities did. All that Xoom required was that you place a link to the Xoom site, which could be tastefully done by adding a statement to the effect that "The author expresses her appreciation...," with a simple text link to the Xoom site.

Xoom was also easy to use. Not only were a wider variety of file types supported for upload, but Carol could also edit her files offline. Other servers require editing online. The problem with online editing is that if there is a service interruption to your connection, you lose your changes and have to start over again.

Marketing the Web resume's URL

Carol used several mechanisms for getting people to her Web resume. But the three she found the most useful were employer matching services, search engines, and her paper resume. Each involved special considerations in marketing her Web resume.

Employer matching services

The primary way that people found her Web resume was through employer matching services that were narrowly tailored to her desired employment-search as a senior employee benefits attorney. BenefitsLink (`http://www.benefitslink.com`) was by far the most effective because it focused on employee benefits issues.

This service provided another advantage: Carol was able to insert a piece of HTML code into the online resume submission form, which created a hyperlink from the match service directly to her Web resume. In the case of BenefitsLink, she enclosed the description of her resume—senior employee benefits attorney—with the link tags, creating a clickable link to her Web resume (see Chapter 9 for a refresher on how to create these links.) Thus, when you scrolled down the list of available candidates on one of the BenefitsLink pages, you were presented with a direct link to her Web resume for additional information.

Another alternative was to simply include the URL of her Web resume somewhere in the online resume submission forms, just as you would include it on a paper resume. The advantage is that recruiters have the option of copying and pasting the URL into a Web browser. This is especially useful when a URL is very long, and typos are possible.

After she had posted her resume to one of these employer matching services, she logged in to see how her final submission looked.

Search engines

Alta Vista (http://www.altavista.com) generated the most traffic in the shortest amount of time to Carol's Web resume, an important consideration in the short time frame that she had for her job search. Alta Vista typically indexes new URLs within a couple of days after they are submitted, rather than several weeks as is usually the case with other search engines.

Another advantage to using Alta Vista is that anything submitted to Alta Vista was also searchable on Yahoo! (http://www.yahoo.com).

Carol also discovered—too late for her online resume, but in time for use with the client-development site she later constructed—a way to get materials instantly into the Infoseek index (http://www.infoseek.com). Pages on most of the free Web servers (e.g., Xoom, GeoCities, or AOL) can be indexed in Infoseek only by sending an e-mail to Infoseek (a process that often takes months).

However, Infoseek itself has recently developed its own free Web page server, called the Web broadcasting service or WBS (http://wbs.com). Pages on WBS can be indexed very quickly on Infoseek (often within minutes). And WBS provides what it calls a "teleporter" service, which allows you to take your Web site on any other server and make a copy of it on WBS just by pressing a button. Thus, she could make a copy of her Xoom site on WBS, and get it into the Infoseek index almost immediately.

Adding separate URLs to other pages linked from her Web resume—not just the home page itself—was also beneficial. For example, if someone found one of her articles online that she had registered separately, the individual would see a "Return to resume" link at the bottom of the article. Thus, this increased Carol's chances of attracting the attention of a potential employer, even if that individual was not specifically looking for resumes.

Integrating the paper resume

The third method was to include the URL to her Web resume at the bottom of her paper resume. All traditional resume development guidelines apply to the paper resume. The URL is an added convenience to refer people to her Web resume for additional information. By doing this, Carol found that this approach was useful even when people had her paper resume, because the online version highlighted some of her skills far more effectively than the paper version.

Measuring the results

To measure the effectiveness of each marketing mechanism, Carol used a free online traffic tracking service that monitored the origin of traffic to her Web resume. She could then use this information to fine-tune the Web resume's design and placement.

Traffic trackers

Carol used Extreme Tracking (`http://extreme-dm.com`) because it provided the most information. The Extreme Tracker statistics pages provided valuable information as to where site traffic originated, how they got there, what kind of browser they were using, and what those elusive keywords are that people choose when searching for her resume.

Carol used this information to fine-tune her Web resume's <META> tags for the search engines, design for the right Web browser, which was Netscape Navigator 2.0, and focus on updating her resume entry at the BenefitsLink Web site.

For example, by analyzing the information that Extreme Tracker provided, Carol was able to determine that BenefitsLink was the most effective mechanism for drawing people to her site and, therefore, she focused her job search efforts on that site. She also realized that it was a good idea to return to that site to update her Web resume, because most of the traffic to her Web resume was coming from the "What's New" page at BenefitsLink, which includes a link to the most recently posted resume.

A little caution—Extreme Tracker requires that you have some knowledge of HTML, because the service requires that you copy and paste HTML into your document using a text editor such as Microsoft Notepad, rather than a WYSIWYG Editor (What You See Is What You Get) like Microsoft FrontPage Express. Many WYSIWYG Editors have a tendency to insert hard returns in unexpected places, where text editors ignore hard returns. This can cause error messages when you insert code required for such things as Web page counters and tracking services.

When choosing a tracker, consider whether to use a free one or one that requires a fee to use. There are many paid counters, starting anywhere from $1 to $14 per month. Mark Welch's site (`http://www.markwelch.com/bannerad/ba_counter.htm`) has one of the most comprehensive lists of both free and pay services. You will need to consider, among other things, whether it would be unprofessional to display a flashy banner add on your otherwise professional Web resume, and whether you consider your resume for personal or commercial uses. (Some free trackers are available only for personal uses.) Carol felt her resume was for commercial uses because in essence, she was advertising her skills for hire.

Link popularity

Another way to measure the exposure of your Web resume is receiving is to test its link popularity. By using search engines to track down referral links, you can get an idea of how "popular" a search engine believes your page to be. That's very important for those engines that rank sites in part by popularity.

Rankings at some search engines are determined in part by the number of Web sites that link to yours. Reason: If other people include links to your site on their own pages, they think it's worth recommending to others. This is the equivalent of "word-of-mouth" advertising on the Web. Don't be afraid to ask others to link to your site, especially if you link to theirs. Reciprocal linking can be a great win-win for both parties.

Search engines can determine the popularity of a page by analyzing how many links there are from other pages. Some engines use this as a means to determine which pages they will include in the index.

This feedback mechanism would be useful in the case of Carol's articles and speeches. When it came time to do a job search using her Web resume, she could test by seeing who was linking to her articles, and then use that information to ensure they link back to her Web resume.

To find out who is linking to your pages, do the following:

Alta Vista

Type the following in Alta Vista's search field: `link:www.articles.com`. This will return all pages in Alta Vista that have a hyperlink containing the following text: `articles.com`. When it came time to do a job search using her Web resume, she could test the link popularity of who was linking to her articles, and use that information to ensure she had a link on those articles that provided people visiting her articles a way to access her Web resume as well.

Excite

Simply enter the URL into the search box and see what comes up.

HotBot

Enter your URL in the search box, and change the default option from "all of the words" to "links to this URL".

Infoseek

Just type in the complete URL and click "Search" from the Infoseek home page. Enter your URL in the "Link" search box without the `http://www` stuff. Instead of entering the entire URL, just enter the domain (`articles.com`, for example).

Play "recruiter for a day"

Another way to determine the effectiveness of your Web resume is to try thinking like a recruiter for a day. When designing or redesigning your site, think about the search queries you want people to use to find it. Then, edit your Web resume so that it is responsive to those queries.

Search for prospective resumes in the search engines that you registered your Web resume to. See what turns up while you search for "prospective" resumes. Use the "view source" feature of your browser to see the HTML tags used, and examine the resumes that scored high in the relevancy ranks.

When you post your resume to a job board, log in as an employer and try searching for your own resume.

Learn how to use Boolean operators to refine your searches. Search engine queries typically return too many or too few hits. These operators, known as Boolean operators use simple words or symbols that instruct a search engine how to conduct searches. Some operators that are common across many of the popular search engines are AND, OR, and NOT which connect words and phrases in the query. Each search engine has its own unique method for using these operators, so be sure to read the instructions carefully.

Think of the keywords that you want people to type to find your resume. If you want people to find you if they type "systems analyst," you should make sure these words appear on your resume. Searching from this point of view will help you to refine the keywords in your Web resume's <META> tags and first few lines of text on the page. For example, Thomas B. Seeker is living in California, and looking for a client server architect position in that state. He may perceive his keywords to be "California, recruitment, high-technology, computer, career, jobs, employment." However, if you shift your perspective to the recruiter's point of view and try to imagine what search terms would lead to your Web resume, you would probably come up with a very different list—for example "Oracle, database, architect, resume."

It is probably a smarter idea that you make sure your Web resume is correctly listed in the engine's indexes, rather than to make it your goal to appear in the top 10 list of every search engine. You are virtually guaranteed to have varying degrees of success. Your goal is target the placement of your resume where your target audience is most likely to find it, and to design it with that target audience in mind.

Jobs Online by Industry

Due to the constant changes of links on the Web, try using your favorite search engine to find the current location of the resources listed below and those listed in the following appendices. Or, try the author's web site at http://www.eresumes.com for continuous updates of the resources listed in these appendices.

Job Boards by Industry

Academic Jobs (Academic Employment Network)
http://www.academploy.com/jobs.cfm

Accounting and Finance (Career Mosaic and AccountingNet)
http://www.accountingjobs.com

Acting and Modeling (Headbooks Online)
http://www.headbooks.com

Acting and Modeling (RGM Productions)
http://www.sheejong.com/rgmprd/actors.html

Administrative Jobs (The Admin Exchange)
http://www.adminexchange.com

Advertising (AdvertisingAge)
http://adage.com/interactive/index.html

Aeronautics (Aero Jobs)
http://www.aerojobs.com

Aerospace Jobs (Space Jobs)
http://www.spacejobs.com

Architectural (CareerPark)
http://www.careerpark.com/jobs/archlist.html

Army, Active Duty, and Army Reserve (US Army Recruiting)
http://www.goarmy.com

Attorney (AttorneyJobs)
http://www.attorneyjobs.com

Attorney (Attorneys @ Work)
http://www.attorneysatwork.com

Automotive (Jobs-careers.com)
http://auto.jobs-careers.com

Aviation, Commercial (The Corporate Aviation Resume Exchange)
http://scendtek.com/care

Bilingual Jobs, English/Asian (Asia-Net)
http://www.asia-net.com

Biotechnology (Medzilla)
http://www.medzilla.com

Broadcasting (TVJobs)
http://www.tvjobs.com

Business Professional (MBA Employment Connection Association)
http://www.mbanetwork.com

Chemistry (Chemistry & Industry Job Database)
http://ci.mond.org/jobs

Christian (ChristianNet)
http://www.christianet.com

Coaching, Football (COACH)
http://www.coachhelp.com

College Graduate (Adguide's College Recruiter Employment Site)
http://www.adguide.com

College Graduate (Career Mosaic)
http://www.careermosaic.com

College Graduate (JobCenter)
http://www.jobcenter.com

College Graduate (JobDirect)
http://www.jobdirect.com

College Graduate (Jobtrak)
http://www.jobtrak.com

College Graduate (JobWeb)
http://www.jobweb.org

College Graduate (Stanford's The Job Resource)
http://www.thejobresource.com

College Graduate, MBAs (MBA Job)
http://www.mbajob.com

Computing (Computerwork.com)
http://www.computerwork.com

Computing (Job Engine)
http://www.jobengine.com

Computing (The Computer Jobs Store)
http://www.computerjobs.com

Computing (The National Computer Jobs Store)
http://www.national.computerjobs.com

Contract Employment (Contract Employment eXchange)
http://www.cex.com

Contract Employment Jobs (National Technical Employment Services)
http://www.ntes.com

Contract Employment (Net-Temps)
http://www.net-temps.com

**Construction
(Architecture Engineering Construction InfoCenter)**
http://www.aecinfo.com/classifi/helpwant.html

Construction (Engineering News Record)
http://www.enr.com

Culinary (StarChefs)
http://www.starchefs.com

Education (Higheredjobs Online)
http://www.higheredjobs.com

Education (The Chronicle of Higher Education)
http://chronicle.com/jobs

Education (The Education JobSite)
http://www.edjobsite.com

Electronics Industry (TechJobBank)
http://www.techjobbank.com

**Emergency Service
(National Directory of Emergency Services)**
http://www1.policejobs.com/ndes

Engineering Jobs, Contract (ContractEngineering.com)
http://www.contractengineering.com

Engineering Jobs, Permanent (EngineeringJobs.com)
http://www.engineeringjobs.com

Environmental (Environmental Careers, Inc.)
http://www.environmentalcareers.com

**Environmental
(National Registry of Environmental Professionals)**
http://www.nrep.org

European Jobs (EuroJobs)
http://www.eurojobs.com

**Executive and Professional Jobs for Adults Over Forty
(Forty Plus of Northern California)**
http://www.sirius.com/~40plus

Executive Jobs, Asia (Executive Access, Hong Kong)
http://www.hk.net/~eal/index.html

Executive Jobs for Ethnic Minorities
http://www.ethnicity.com

Executive Jobs (Technology Registry)
http://www.techreg.com

Experienced Professionals, All Industries (American Jobs)
http://www.americanjobs.com

Experienced Professionals, All Industries (PursuitNet)
http://www.pursuit.com/jobs

Fashion (Fashion Net)
http://www.fashion.net

Financial (Michael Muller, Executive Recruiter)
http://www.financialjobs.com/fobf.html

Fitness (FitLife)
http://www.fitlife.com

Funerary (FuneralNet)
http://www.funeralnet.com

General Employment (NationJob's Specialty Pages)
http://www.nationjob.com/frqsrc.html

**General Employment, Search by Company, State, or Industry
(The Internet Job Source)**
http://www.statejobs.com

**General Employment, Search by Location, Industry, or Function
(Recruiting-Links.Com)**
http://www.recruiting-links.com

Government Jobs, Federal (Federal Jobs Digest)
http://www.jobsfed.com

Government Jobs, Federal (FedWorld)
http://www.fedworld.gov

Government Jobs, Federal (Office of Personnel Management)
http://www.usajobs.opm.gov

Government Jobs, Public Service (Jobs in Government)
http://www.jobsingovernment.com

Government Jobs, Public Service (Public Service Employees Network)
http://www.pse-net.com

Grocery (The Produce Job Exchange)
http://www.producejobs.com

Health Care (America's HealthCareSource)
http://www.healthcaresource.com

Health Care (Career Mosaic's HealthOpps)
http://www.healthopps.com

Health Care (HealthCareerWeb)
http://www.healthcareerweb.com

Health Care (Medzilla)
http://www.medzilla.com

Health Care (Physicians Employment)
http://www.physemp.com

Health Care (Physicians Online Network)
http://www.po.com

High-Technology (CareerMosaic)
http://www.careermosaic.com

High-Technology (DICE)
http://www.dice.com

**High-Technology Jobs for Women
(Women in Technology International)**
http://www.witi.com

**High-Technology
(Westech's Virtual Job Fair's Searchable Database)**
http://www.vjf.com

Horticulture (Ferrell's Jobs in Horticulture)
http://wwww.hortjobs.com

Hospitality (HospitalityNet Virtual Job Exchange)
http://www.hospitalitynet.nl/job/opport.htm

Human Resources, Benefits Administration (BenefitsLink)
http://www.benefitslink.com

Human Resources (CareerPark)
http://www.careerpark.com/jobs/humalist.html

Human Resources (Recruiting Options)
http://www.recruitingoptions.net

Human Resources, Training and Development (TCM's HR Careers)
http://www.tcm.com/hr-careers/career

Information Technology (Communications Week)
http://techweb.cmp.com/cw/ccareers/jobs.html

Information Technology (Computerworld Careers)
http://careers.computerworld.com

**Information Technology Jobs for Older Adults
(The Senior Staff Job Information Databank)**
http://www.srstaff.com

Information Technology (LAN Times)
http://www.lantimes.com/careers/job-board.html

Insurance (Career Mosaic's The Insurance Career Center)
http://www.connectyou.com/talent

Insurance (The Digital Financier)
http://www.dfin.com

Internet (Bay Area Coolware Classifieds)
http://www.jobsjobsjobs.com

Internet Technology (Seybold Seminars Online Jobbank)
http://www.supersite.net/seyboldjobbank

Jobs for International Physicians Who Want to Work in the U.S. (Physicians RecruitNet)
http://www.physiciannet.com

Jobs for People with Security Clearances (Classified Employment Web Site)
http://www.yourinfosource.com

Land Professional (Right of Way)
http://www.rightofway.com

Legal (LawJobs)
http://www.lawjobs.com

Legal (Law Journal listings)
http://www.ljextra.com/public/lawjobs/lawjoblistings.html

Legal Secretary Jobs (Personnel at Law)
http://personnelatlaw.com

Mechanical Engineering (MechanicalEngineer.com)
http://www.mechanicalengineer.com

Mechanical Engineering (The American Society of Mechanical Engineers)
http://www.asme.org/memagazine/index.html

Military Transition (Army Career and Alumni Program)
http://www.acap.army.mil

Military Transition (Center for Employment Management)
http://www.cemjob.com

Military Transition (Clarke & Associates)
http://www.jclarke.com

Military Transition (Corporate Gray Online)
http://www.bluetogray.com

Military Transition (HIRE Quality)
http://www.hire-quality.com

Military Transition (Transition Assistance Online)
http://www.taonline.com/cgi-bin/showpositions.exe

Nanny (Nanny Jobs USA)
http://www.ilovemynanny.com/jobs

Natural Resources (Cyber-Sierra's Natural Resources Job Search)
http://www.cyber-sierra.com/nrjobs

Navy (US Navy)
http://www.navyjobs.com

News
http://www.newsjobs.com/jbanks.html

Nonprofit (GoodWorks at Tripod)
http://www.tripod.com/work/goodworks/search.html

Nonprofit (Philanthropy Journal Online)
http://philanthropy-journal.org

Nursing (VirtualNurse)
http://virtualnurse.com

Outdoor (CoolWorks)
http://www.coolworks.com

Pharmaceutical (International Pharmajobs)
http://www.pharmajobs.com

Pharmacy (Pharmacy Week)
http://www.pweek.com/jobs.html

Physicians (Physicians Employment)
http://www.physemp.com

Physics (PhysicsWeb)
http://physicsweb.org

Pollution Prevention (Pollution Online)
http://www.pollutiononline.com

Programming (Jobs for Programmers)
http://www.jfpresources.com

Radiology and Oncology (IntraVision)
http://www.intravsn.com

Recording Industry (Los Angeles Music Network)
http://www.lamn.com

Research (Gallup)
http://www.gallup.com/jobs.htm

Semiconductor Industry (CircuitOnline)
http://www.circuitonline.com

Social Service (SocialService.com)
http://socialservice.com/index.htm

Social Service (The New Social Worker Online)
http://www.socialworker.com/career.htm

Software Development (developers.net)
http://www.developers1.net

Space Jobs (Space Careers)
http://www.spacelinks.com/SpaceCareers/Careers.html

Sports Jobs (CBS SportsLine)
http://www.sportsline.com

Summer Camp (CoolWorks)
http://www.coolworks.com/showme/campjobs.htm

Teaching (Department of Defense)
http://www.odedodea.edu

Teaching (K-12 Jobs.com)
http://www.k12jobs.com

Teaching, Language (Employment Resources for Language Teachers)
http://www.tcom.ohiou.edu/OU_Language/teacher/job.html#Web

Teaching (NationJob Network)
http://www.nationjob.com/education

Teaching (Teachers @ Work)
http://www.teachersatwork.com

Teaching (The Teacher's Employment Network)
http://www.teachingjobs.com

Teaching (Teaching Jobs Overseas)
http://www.hevanet.com/pcis/index.htm

Telecommuting for Programmers (Jobs for Programmers)
http://www.jfpresources.com/jobtele1.html

Telecommuting (TelecommutingJobs)
http://www.tjobs.com

Television Industry (MediaLine)
http://monet.carmelnet.com/ml/jobs.phtml

Truck Driver Jobs (Layover.com)
http://www.layover.com

Truck Driver Jobs (TruckNet)
http://www.trucknet.com

Volunteering (Internet Nonprofit Center)
http://www.nonprofits.org/parlor/list.html

Volunteering (Virtual Volunteering)
http://www.impactonline.org

Volunteering (Volunteer 101 Online)
http://www.volunteer101.org

Water Resources (Universities Water Information Network)
http://www.uwin.siu.edu/announce/jobs

Webmastering (Seybold Seminars Online Jobbank)
http://www.supersite.net/seyboldjobbank

Webmastering (Webmaster's Guild)
http://www.webmaster.org

Web Professional (The Web Career Research Center)
http://www.cio.com/forums/wmf_job_posts.html

Writing (The Write Job)
http://www.writerswrite.com/jobs

Metajob boards

America's Job Bank
http://www.ajb.dni.us
America's Job Bank is a partnership between the U.S. Department of Labor and the Public Employment Service. The Public Employment Service is a program that provides labor exchange service to employers and job seekers through a network of 1,800 offices throughout the United States.

BridgePath.com
http://www.bridgepath.com
The emphasis is on placing employees quickly using convenient methods to send job announcements tailored to your skills and interests

c|net search.com
http://www.search.com (select "Employment" category)
Search more than 30 different job boards one at a time, but all in one place.

The California Gold Talent Bank
http://www.webcom.com/~career/crtb.html
A fee-based service of the California Career and Employment Center, the goal is to build a Talent Bank where California employers and recruiting professionals can locate qualified job-candidates who are seeking employment. The California Resume/Talent Bank is keyword-searchable for fast and easy access by employers and recruiting professionals. A unique feature is that they also provide you with

the URL of your resume so that you can direct potential employers to your resume without having to conduct a keyword search to find it.

The Career Builder Network

`http://www.careerbuilder.com`

Lets you target your job search on dozens of the best career sites. These sites are categorized as Broad Appeal Sites, Diversity Sites, Industry Sites, and Professional Sites. You can also register a Personal Search Agent at each site.

Career Central

`http://www.careercentral.com`

For experienced MBAs, software developers, and marketing professionals.

CareerCity

`http://www.careercity.com`

Specializing in technical and professional jobs, CareerCity is operated by Adams Media Corporation, publishers of the popular *Knock 'em Dead* and *JobBank* series of career books.

CareerFile

`http://www.careerfile.com`

All free, this is a searchable library of executive, managerial and technical talent and thousands of employers.

CareerMagazine

`http://careermag.com`

CareerMagazine has its own resume bank available to Web surfers. It contains resumes of job-seekers submitted to NCS and downloaded daily from the major Internet newsgroups. These resume postings are searchable by location, job title and/or skills required. Resumes are posted for a six-month period, available to employers and recruiters worldwide.

CareerMart

`http://www.careermart.com`

Search jobs by state, region, job category, and company. By registering for CareerMart's e-mail agent service, you will automatically be notified via e-mail of matching job descriptions as they become available. A Virtual Conference Center highlights selected career topics where individuals are invited to participate in online job fairs, intervieiws, or simply join in the discussion with industry employers.

CareerMosaic

`http://www.careermosaic.com`

A favorite first stop for recruiters, this online career clearinghouse provides a flexible form for posting your resume. Resumes can be posted for up to 90 days by pasting an ASCII text-only version in the form provided.

CareerParadise
http://www.emory.edu/CAREER

Maintained by Emory University in Atlanta, this site includes candid reviews and links of other online career resource centers.

CareerPath
http://www.careerpath.com

Search newspaper employment ads from eight major cities. Access *The Boston Globe*; *The Los Angeles Times*; *The New York Times*; *Philadelphia Inquirer*; *The San Jose Mercury News*; *South Florida Sun-Sentinel*; and *The Washington Post*. CareerPath requires registration to post your resume. Set aside some time, because filling out the form is not as easy as it may seem.

CareerSite
http://www.careersite.com

Specializes in confidential job searches. You can also search for jobs that match your particular profile.

CareerWeb
http://www.cweb.com

Store your resume online. Complete the online nomination form once, store it, then apply for all jobs easier and faster. Section provided to include a cover letter.

CEO Express!
http://www.ceoexpress.com

A meta-site of useful links and career information for business leaders.

HeadHunter.net
http://www.headhunter.net

This very popular employment site boasts free resume posting and free job postings.

Help Wanted.com
http://www.helpwanted.com

Submit your resume as an HTML document. Your resume will remain posted for 60 days before it expires. Includes a field to submit the URL of your personal Web page.

Jobs & Adverts
http://www.ja-usa.com

A unique site that offers jobs, advertising, and information to people of many nationalities. If you are looking for a job in the international market, this is where you can find up-to-date career opportunities.

Job Engine
http://www.jobengine.com

Search and post your resume in a comprehensive, nationwide listing of employment opportunities, sponsored by Ziff-Davis Publishing.

JobOptions

http://www.joboptions.com

Formerly known as E.span, this site allows you to post your resume by either pasting in an existing one or completing a more comprehensive form and letting JobOptions format one for you. Important to note that you will need a resume title— use something distinctive like a phrase from your job objective here. Once posted, JobOptions lets you know how many times your resume has been viewed. You can also use the Job Agent to receive postings via e-mail.

JobSmart

http://www.jobsmart.org

No career-oriented list of Web sites is complete without a reference to this exceptional resource. Originally specializing in job-search resources in California, it is now expanding nationwide. This site was awarded the *American Library Association's Gale Research Award for Excellence in Reference & Adult Services.* This award is given to one project each year, and was the first time it was given to a Web site.

JobTrak

http://www.jobtrak.com

A job board for college students and alumni.

Med Search

http://www.medsearch.com

Specializing in jobs for medical professionals, this site boasts a career center, bulletin board, news group, and employment site all rolled into one.

The Monster Board

http://www.monster.com

Just as its name implies, this behemoth of a Web site has thousands of jobs listed in both technical and nontechnical fields, organized nationally and internationally. After submitting your resume, you can sign up for the job search agent and have job offerings e-mailed to you directly.

NationJob Network

http://www.nationjob.com

With the assistance of P.J. Scout, this free service automatically sends you new jobs that match your choices via e-mail. This site also lists several unique specialty pages where you can narrow your job search by a specific industry.

Online Career Center

http://www.occ.com

OCC is one of the few career sites that allows you to submit a resume in HTML. You can type in or copy and paste the HTML directly into the form. Be sure to test all of your hyperlinks, especially if you plan on including images in your resume, before submitting it.

Recruiters Online Network (RON)

http://www.ipa.com/careers/resumemail.html

A unique service for introducing yourself to a member recruiter. The Recruiters Online Network (formerly the Internet Professional Association), RON is a worldwide virtual community of employment firms. Post your resume via the online form provided. A very straightforward process compared to earlier versions.

Talent Scout

http://www.talentscout.com

Operated by the *San Jose Mercury News*, this job board is the gateway to jobs in the Silicon Valley.

The Wall Street Journal

http://www.careers.wsj.com

A job board that specializes in executive, managerial, and professional jobs with a database that is updated twice weekly

Yahoo! Employment Classifieds

http://www.yahoo.com

By entering the keywords "employment classifieds" in Yahoo's search field, you can access job postings and resumes by industry.

Appendix B

Online Research

Company directories

Before you can take advantage of online job ads for a specific company, first find out if they have a corporate Web site. Refer to the following company directories to browse thousands of corporate Web sites by alphabetical listing.

Companies Online
http://www.companiesonline.com
Sponsored by Dun & Bradstreet and Lycos, this site allows you to search more than 60,000 public and private companies by industry.

Gateway to Associations Online
http://www.asaenet.org/gateway/onlineassocslist.html
Sponsored by the American Society of Association Executives, this site lets you search by name or browse a directory of associations currently operating on the Web.

The Government by Sterby
http://www.erols.com/irasterb/gov.htm
Find about everything you ever needed to know about the Federal government here.

Hoover's Corporate Web Site
http://www.hoovers.com
Browse thousands of corporate home pages by alphabetical listing.

The Riley Guide's Tell Me About This Employer
http://www.dbm.com/jobguide/research.html
An exhaustive resource for conducting detailed corporate research online.

Yahoo! Company Job Listings
http://www.yahoo.com
This is gold! An exhaustive array of jobs are listed here with direct links to corporate job listings (search by keywords "company job listings").

Discussion forums by industry

Following is a sampling of the kinds of discussion forums and topics you can find on the Internet. To refine your research further, try the metaresearch tools at the end of this list.

About Work Discussion Boards
http://www.aboutwork.com/messageboards
Ask the experts and talk to other college graduates on these forums, which cover topics such as getting a job, being out of work, and career strategies.

Advertising Age's marketing and advertising forums
Discussion topics include:

Digital Media
http://adage.com/interactions/digital

Customer Loyalty
http://adage.com/interactions/loyalty

Marketing
http://adage.com/interactions/marketing

Branding
http://adage.com/interactions/branding

Censorship
http://adage.com/interactions/censorship

Web Statistics
http://adage.com/interactions/statistics

Electronic Commerce
http://adage.com/interactions/commerce

Agriculture Discussion Forums and Mailing Lists
http://www.oneglobe.com/agriculture/newslist.html
Discuss agribusiness, agriculture, and farming issues.

Amazon City's Networking Forum
http://www.amazoncity.com/professional
This networking forum is a chance to talk with other women about career, business, and becoming an entrepreneur.

Blacksmithing Techniques Forum
http://www.fantasyforge.com
Tips for the Blacksmithing industry (select "Links" from the home page to go to the forum). Post your tips or ask questions.

Builder Online's Builders Forums

http://www.builderonline.com

Meet homeowners, builders, and remodelers to discuss topics such as construction tips, design, and marketing homes (select "Talk" from the index bar).

Business (BizProWeb)

http://www.bizproweb.com

Access business and professional newsgroups, as well as a collection of interactive bulletin boards with topics including: small business; accounting and finance (bookkeeping, financial software, accounting techniques); marketing and promotion; and home office concerns, among others.

Business Contact Forum-Export and Import

http://www.lengua.com/wwwboard/wwwboard.html

A forum for people who are looking for new international business partners.

CCIM Commercial Real Estate Network Forums

http://www.ccim.com/entryway.html

Public forums are available for property marketing and open discussion. The Career Resources forum is an excellent place find job postings in commercial investment real estate.

Culinary (Epicurious Food)

http://www.epicurious.com

Talk about everything from eating and drinking to playing with your food (select *Forums* from the index bar).

Cyber Cyclery's Bicyclists and Bicycle Messenger Forums

http://www.cycling.org

Access discussion forums for bicycle enthusiasts and bicycle messengers. Cyber Cyclery has more than 100,000 visitors every month and well over 20,000 bicyclists subscribed to the more than 200 electronic mailing lists.

Education (Classroom Electric)

http://www.sol.com.sg/classroom/newsgrps.html

A listing of Usenet newsgroups that may be relevant to educators.

Electronic Engineering Times online special interest groups

These are special interest groups (SIGs) which are great resources for keeping tabs on the latest in this industry:

Communications SIG

http://techweb.cmp.com/eet/com/eecom1.html

Electronic Design Automation SIG

http://techweb.cmp.com/eet/eda/eda.html

Entrepreneur Magazine's Small Business Forum

http://www.entrepreneurmag.com/forum.hts

Entrepreneurs discuss a variety of topics from starting a business to managing current operations.

Environmental News Network Forum

http://www.enn.com/community

Forum discussing a variety of environmental themes.

Fast Company Forums

http://www.fastcompany.com/community

Get connected with readers of *Fast Company*, a magazine that explores new practices shaping how work gets done.

Healthcare Forums

http://www.healthcareforums.com

A comprehensive listing of forums where you can interact with other healthcare professionals from around the world.

History Forums

http://www.federalist.com

A comprehensive resource guide to discussion forums, called "ports," where you can meet other like-minded people with an interest in American History.

Home-Based Business Forums

http://homebasedbusiness.com/cgibin/index.cgi

Discuss tips, strategies, secrets, and ideas for the home and small business entrepreneur.

Human Resources (Workinfo.com) Forum

http://www.workinfo.com

A human resources, training, and industrial relations discussion forum.

Inc. Magazine

http://www.inc.com/peertopeer

Discussions of small business startups, marketing, technology, and industry information for entrepreneurs.

Jobs (Get A Job)

http://www.getajob.com/newsgrps.html

A comprehensive listing of newsgroups related to finding jobs by geographic location.

Law Enforcement (Jane's Police Forum)

http://www.janes.com/police/polforset.html

A professional forum where you can discuss your opinions on any issue concerning law enforcement

The Legal Domain Network

http://www.kentlaw.edu/lawnet/lawnet.html

A substantial number of law-related discussion lists. Created as a joint venture between several law schools.

Money Magazine/Boards

http://www.pathfinder.com

Forum dedicated to finance and business (select "Boards" from the index bar of the Welcome page).

The Motley Fool Message Boards

http://boards.fool.com/Folders.asp

Discussions of stocks, finance, investments, and other financial issues.

Nursing Listservs and Usenet Newsgroups

http://www.nursingworld.org/listserv/index.htm

An easy-to-browse list of special interest groups for the nursing industry.

Nursing (Virtual Nurse Interactive)

http://virtualnurse.com/interactive.html

Discussion forums, interactive polls, and regularly scheduled live chats with other nurses.

Psych Central Mailing Lists

http://www.grohol.com/mail.htm

Mailing list index for support group moderators, as well as professionals in psychological services.

Television Forums

http://www.tvjobs.com/net_for.htm

Communicate with others in the television industry.

Third Age Media

http://www.thirdage.com

In this virtual community, connect with other older adults who have gone beyond raising a family and pursuing a career.

Travel Forums

http://www.traveloco.com/forums/index.asp

Discuss everything under the sun relating to travel and the travel industry. Join a community and build a free Web page.

The Washington Post Business Talk

http://www.washingtonpost.com

Discuss a wide variety of topics ranging from business, international news, sports, and entertainment (select "Talk Central" from the index bar).

Web Development Professionals
(Professional Presence Network Forum)
http://www.ppn.org

Discuss everything from graphic design, Internet marketing, Web-site design, and professional ethics in the industry.

Web Marketing Forum
http://www.wilsoninet.com/hn/forum

Forum hosted by Wilson Internet Services that addresses strategies and experience in Web marketing.

Sources for finding corporate URLs and e-mail addresses

BigFoot
http://www.bigfoot.com

An e-mail and phone directory. Build your own electronic address book to capture the business listings you use most frequently. A great tool to research and track your employment contacts.

Bigyellow
http://www.bigyellow.com

Find people, businesses and e-mail addresses. Includes yellow pages for Africa, Asia, the Middle East, Australia, New Zealand, Europe, North America, and South and Central America.

Four11
http://www.four11.com

Internet e-mail directory; provides features to initiate net phone conversations online.

InfoSpace People Search
http://www.infospace.com

Find people, places, and things. Provides useful links to city guides and offers background check services.

Internet Public Library
http://www.ipl.org/ref/RR/static/bus1570.html

Links to international business directories.

LinkStar
http://www.linkstar.com

Directory of Web sites, personal addresses, and businesses.

Snap!
http://www.snap.com

Features an e-mail lookup, along with white and yellow pages sections.

Switchboard
http://www.switchboard.com

Find people, businesses, e-mail, and Web sites. Search for residential phone numbers. Register for free e-mail and Web pages.

The Ultimate White Pages
http://www.theultimates.com/white

Use this resource to search the major search directories all in one place.

WhoWhere
http://www.whowhere.com

Find people and e-mail addresses. Also sign up for free e-mail and Web pages. Includes links to find jobs and post your resume.

WWW Virtual Reference Sites
http://www.dreamscape.com/frankvad/reference-business.html

Gateway to access thousands of the most popular information reference locations on the Web including maps, facts, calculators, dictionaries, chat, and jobs. Also includes people, e-mail, phone numbers, and news searching features.

ZD Net's Company Finder
http://search.zdnet.com/cgi-bin/texis/cofinder/cofinder

Search for computer companies.

Metatools for discussion forums

Try one of these metareseach tools search for newsgroups, mailing lists, and discussion forums for any area of interest. The chances are that you'll find hundreds of people talking about your area of expertise!

CataList
http://www.lsoft.com/lists/listref.html

Browse this catalog of over 20,000 public LISTSERV mailing lists on the Internet by catagory.

Deja News
http://www.dejanews.com

Search mailing lists.

Forum One
http://www.forumone.com

Search Web-based discussion forums.

The LISZT
http://www.liszt.com

Search Usenet newsgroups.

Publicly Accessible Mailing Lists (PAML)

http://www.neosoft.com/internet/paml

PAML is an extensive database of mailing lists for either browsing or searching. This site includes excellent information on how to subscribe and unsubscribe to mailing lists.

Tile.NET

http://tile.net/listserv

Provides a search utility for locating Internet discussion groups by name, subject, country, and sponsoring organization.

USBBS List

http://www.channel1.com/usbbs/index.cgi

A list of PC Bulletin Boards in the United States.

Usenet Information Launch Pad

http://sunsite.unc.edu/usenet-i/home.html

Search for a newsgroup by entering a text string. Also extensive links to other useful pages including Usenet FAQs.

News by industry

AdvertisingAge

http://adage.com/news_and_features/index.html

Daily headline news in the marketing and advertising industry.

Builders Online

http://www.builderonline.com/builder/news

Daily headline news in the building industry.

The Chronicle of Higher Education

http://chronicle.com/chronicle

Top stories in academia.

CNN Financial Network

http://cnnfn.com

Daily news updates on business and finance topics.

Computer News Daily

http://computernewsdaily.com

The New York Times Syndicate.

Education Week on the Web

http://www.edweek.org/context/clips/clips.htm

Daily round-up of education news and articles from around the nation. Updated daily after noon, Eastern Standard Time.

Electronic Engineering Times
http://techweb.cmp.com/eet/823/hr.html

Daily headline news in the electronic engineering and technology management industry.

Electronic Recruiting News
http://www.interbiznet.com/hrstart.html

Front-page news on the recruiting industry.

Entertainment News Daily
http://entertainmentnewsdaily.com

The New York Times Syndicate.

Environmental NewsLink
http://www.caprep.com/new_dig3.htm

Daily news digest for a wide variety of environmental media topics.

Gary Johnson's BraveNewWorkWorld Work News
http://www.newwork.com

Keep up with the future of work; updated daily.

Health News Daily
http://yourhealthdaily.com

The New York Times Syndicate.

Inc. Online
http://www.inc.com/incmagazine

Use the easy *Inc.* Online Quick Search field to find news stories by industry for executive and small business management.

Internet Press
http://gallery.uunet.be/internetpress/link40.htm

A meta gateway resource for news and press releases from around the world.

Media Central
http://www.mediacentral.com/Magazines/MediaDaily

Follow the daily news that shapes the media industry.

NewsPage
http://www.newspage.com

Daily news on everything imaginable. Customize your own personal news page.

Philanthropy Journal Online
http://www.pj.org

National headline news on philanthropy, fundraising, foundation, and nonprofit industries. Subscribe to a free weekly e-mail newsletter for the nonprofit sector (http://www.philanthropy-journal.org/front/front.htm).

Pollution Online
`http://news.pollutiononline.com/industry-news/index/page1.html`
Current news for the pollution equipment and pollution control industry.

PR Newswire
`http://www.prnewswire.com`
A database of stories appearing on PR Newswire from various companies. Read the Company News On-Call (`http://www.prnewswire.com/cnoc/cnoc.html`) and Feature News (`http://www.prnewswire.com/features/feature.html`) for details on specific companies.

Psychology
`http://www.wiso.uni-augsburg.de/sozio/hartmann/psycho/journals.html`
Extensive links to psychological journals.

The Red Herring
`http://www.herring.com/mag`
Current business information for the technology and entertainment industries.

The San Jose Mercury News' Mercury Center
`http://www.sjmercury.com`
Headline news on technology trends in the Silicon Valley.

TechWire
`http://www.techweb.com/wire/wire.html`
Daily headline news in the high-tech industry.

TechWire's Internet Daily
`http://www.techweb.com/wire/online/online.html`
Daily headline news in the Internet market segment of the high-tech industry.

Travel Hacker
http://www.travelfinder.com
Articles, news, and services for travel agents.

Upside
`http://www.upside.com`
The latest insights on the people and companies shaping the digital era.

USA Today
`http://www.usatoday.com`
National headline news at a glance.

The Washington Post
`http://www.washingtonpost.com`
Headline news on government trends in the Nation's capitol.

Metatools for news

Try one of these metaresearch tools to search for additional industry news resources:

American City Business Journals
http://www.amcity.com
Browse top business headlines from over 35 business journals.

E&P MediaInfo Links
http://www.mediainfo.com/emedia
Search for news by geographic location and media type such as city guides, associations, newspapers, magazines, radio, syndicated news services, or television.

IndustryLink
http://www.industrylink.com
A comprehensive directory with links to dozens of industry-specific Web sites.

Industry Research Desk
http://www.virtualpet.com/industry/mfg/mfg.htm
Research Web sites for specific industries.

Infoseek's IndustryWatch
http://www.industrywatch.com
Monitor daily headlines by industry all from one convenient Web page.

NewsCentral
http://www.all-links.com/newscentral
Search for newspapers worldwide.

Starting Point
http://www.stpt.com/magazine/magazine.html
Use the PowerSearch Magazine tool to search magazines found on the Web.

Supernews
http://www.supernews.com
A super gateway for searching articles and reading newsgroups.

Transium Business Intelligence
http://www.transium.com
Research over 300,000 company profiles by company name or stock symbol. Also features over 1 million articles compiled from leading business and trade publications.

Virtual job fairs

CFG, Inc.
http://www.cfg-inc.com
Specializes in career fairs for the information technology, information systems, engineering, sales, management, and business professionals.

The JobWeb's Search Career Fairs
http://www.jobweb.org/search/cfairs

A career fair clearinghouse sponsored by member colleges of the National Association of Colleges and Employers.

The Lendman Group
http://www.lendman.com

This group has many years of experience in producing career fairs.

The Monster Board Career Fair Information
http://www.monster.com

Provides a calendar of career fair information.

NetWORK Events
http://www.cfcjobs.com

A high-tech career fair for those looking for jobs in the computer, semiconductor, engineering, telecommunications and information technology industries.

Professional Exchange
http://www.professional-exchange.com

Career fair for high-tech professionals, including high-tech sales professionals.

SENET Career Expo
http://www.senetcareer.com

Specializes in high-tech and sales and management career fairs.

Westech's Virtual Job Fair
http://www.careerexpo.com

A California-based corporation, has specialized in high technology career events and publications nationally since 1982.

Other online job search resources

About Work's Workstyle Quiz
http://www.aboutwork.com/quiz/workstyle

Find out how your personality affects your workstyle by taking this simple quiz.

Ask An Expert
http://www.askanexpert.com/askanexpert/index.html

Experts from many different fields answer your questions via e-mail.

Discovering your Career in Business
http://www.careerdiscovery.com

Doctors Timothy Butler and James Waldroop, directors of career development programs at the Harvard Business School, offer a CareerLeader guided tour, which is a virtual tour that guides you through your own business career self-assessment program.

InfoHub's Time Zone Converter
http://www.infohub.com/TRAVEL/AID/timezone.html

Convert between national and international time zones.

Internet Travel Agency, Inc.
http://www.internettravelagency.com

Research online and obtain some of the lowest airfare for that upcoming interview or corporate relocation house-hunting trip.

Ivillage Career Experts
http://www.ivillage.com/experts/career.html

Join in on several channels to access career and workplace experts online.

JobHunt
http://www.job-hunt.org

A metalist of online job search resources and services.

MapQuest
http://www.mapquest.com

An interactive worldwide road atlas. Find out how to get anywhere.

StudentCenter.com
http://www.studentcenter.com

A great resource to practice your interviewing skills.

The Interview Network
http://www.pse-net.com/interview/interview.htm

Provides links to links to more than 1,000 possible interview questions for various professions and more than 600 questions categorized by job function.

200 Letters for Job Hunters
http://www.careerlab.com/letters/default.htm

Your online resource for over 200 sample cover letters from responding to a want ad and follow-up, to negotiating a pay raise and resigning gracefully.

World Times and Dialing Codes
http://www.whitepages.com.au/time.shtml

Search by county or state to find time and area code information.

Women's Wire Find Your Niche
http://www.womenswire.com/quiz/careers

The quiz opens with these statistics: "According to a recent Women's Wire poll, 53 percent of women work primarily to pay the bills. Only 33 percent feel their work is an important part of who they are." Take this brief quiz to find your niche.

Yahoo!'s Currency Converter
`http://quote.yahoo.com/m5?a=1&s=USD&t=JPY`

The latest rates for a variety of international currency. If you don't want to type in the above URL, simply search on the keywords "currency converter" in the Yahoo! search field.

Resume writing resources

Archeus
`http://www.golden.net/~archeus/resserv.htm`

Start your research by reading this page on selecting a resume writing service and browse this list of resume articles found on the Web.

JobSmart's Selected Resume Resources on the Web
`http://jobsmart.org/tools/resume/res-web.htm`

The ultimate resource on how to write and where to send resumes.

Professional Association of Resume Writers (PARW)
`http://www.parw.com`

An online directory of member professional resume writing services.

Resumania
`http://www1.umn.edu/ohr/ecep/resume/resume.htm`

An award-winning interactive workbook that presents the basics of resume writing.

Yana Parker's Damn Good Resume Web Site
`http://www.damngood.com/jobseekers/skills.html`

If you are having trouble identifying your special skills, talents, and abilities, try one of these self-help quizzes.

Resume writing and posting services

A Better Word & Resume
`http://www.saber.net/~abetterword`

A certified professional resume writer (CPRW), Nancy Karvonen has over 15 years of experience in resume writing and job-search consulting.

Acorn Career Counseling and Resume Writing
`http://www.acornresume.com/Acorn.html`

Visit the Resume Doctor who specializes in middle and upper-level management in the high-tech industry. The site offers examples of defective resumes and shows how to fix them.

A+ On-Line Resumes
`http://www.hway.com/olresume`

A lot of good resume examples of liberal arts professionals.

Giselson Writing Services

http://www.gisleson.com

Mark Giselson provides a full range of career-related services to clients nationwide. His credits include Pati Gelfman's Minnesota Job Seekers' Sourcebook, and Joyce Lain Kennedy's Electronic Resume Revolution, Electronic Job Search Revolution, and Resumes for Dummies.

K's Resume Service

http://www.careeravenue.com/net/larocca

Kay and Sam LaRocca and their team of resume writers share their secrets in writing the perfect resume. In addition to tips in improving your resume, they are also uniquely qualified to assist clients with special needs, such as those who have been out of the work force for several years, or who do not have the "required" education but have extensive experience. Visit Kay's monthly advice column on CareerAvenue.

ProType, Ltd

http://members.aol.com/criscito/index.htm

By the author of Barron's *Resumes in Cyberspace*, Pat Criscito, CPRW, is an expert at providing scannable resume services.

Proven Resumes

http://www.provenresumes.com

This one-of-kind resume service specializes in confidence-building, critical to making successful job changes.

Resume Design Services

http://www.erols.com/dilksd/resumedesign.html

This New-Jersey based resume writing firm is proven to be convenient and fast, and gets results.

Resume Factory

http://www.resumefactory.com

A comprehensive resume listing with valuable links to the Web sites of the resume services.

Resume Innovations

http://resume-innovations.com

This service has been doing online resumes for over three years now. A nice search engine.

Resume-Net

http://www.resume-net.com/database.html

Specializes in creating HTML versions of your resume and posting it on their site, announcing it, and posting it confidentially.

Resume Place
http://www.resume-place.com/jobs

Operated by Kathryn Troutman, author of the popular *The Federal Resume Guidebook* and *Reinvention Federal Resumes*, this site provides expert services for all phases of finding Federal government jobs and the job application process.

Shawn's Internet Resume Center
http://www.inpursuit.com/sirc

SIRC specializes in resume services for corporate residents, vice presidents, CFOs, and high-level managers.

Appendix C

Strategies for Creating Keyword Summaries

Before you begin creating your online resume, it's best to review the basics of resume writing as they relate to capturing your skills, accomplishments, and keywords first. That way, you can concentrate on completely on electronic file format and page layout considerations—and not on content.

List your keywords in the order of importance as they appear on your resume. Your resume should contain enough keywords, which are nouns and phrases that high- light technical and professional areas of expertise, industry-related jargon, projects, achievements, special task forces, and other facets of your work history.

Recognize what keywords are:

- Flip through the telephone yellow pages to get a feel for what keywords might apply to your job or industry.
- Scan the "wants" in each of the Want Ads of your local newspaper's employment classifieds section.
- Practice using the card catalog search feature at your local library.
- Test your keyword choice by trying to find other resumes like yours and jobs in your field at the online resume databases and job boards.

Identify the keywords in your resume:

- Take a copy of your resume and highlight those nouns you think the computer might use as keywords in a search.
- Ask yourself whether those keywords adequately describe your work experience and support your job search objectives.

Develop a master keyword log:

- Compile a list of keywords that apply to your particular job title, related job industry, and job responsibilities. This helps to maintain consistency throughout your resume in terms of its content and what you use when posting it online.

- Identify and list specific "buzzwords" that are unique to your job occupation and industry.
- Refer to the *Occupational Outlook Handbook* as a good source of keywords for your particular occupation.

Update your resume to include keywords and a keyword summary:

- Integrate keywords from your master keyword list into your resume.
- Highlight your keywords in the resume's "Keyword Summary" section.

Examples of keyword summaries

The following are sample keyword summaries that illustrate the use of industry-related terms, jargon, and acronyms. A reasonable rule of thumb is to limit the number of keywords from 25 to 35. Their order is determined by their level of importance relative to the position a candidate is applying for. In these examples, the keywords regarding job industry and job titles have the highest level of importance, followed by specific skills, personal traits, ecducation, and work history. Many of these were obtained from classifieds, job descriptions, and actual resumes.

Transportation management professional

General Manager. Assistant General Manager. Regional Distribution Manager. Supervise Drivers. Supervise Personnel Functions. Workers' Compensation. Inbound Operations Management. Freight Operations. LCV. Freight Operations Supervisor. Dockworker Supervisor. Dispatch. DOT Regulations. Training. On-Time Delivery. Backhaul Business. Fleet Maintenance. BA Degree in Economics. Fresno State University.

Police officer

Skilled Negotiator. Police Department. Community Relations. Crisis Management. Emergency. Disaster. Law Enforcement Skills. B.A. in Criminal Justice. University of Southern Oregon.

Small business president; business unit manager

Marketing Manager. Product Manager. Brand Manager. Field Sales. National Sales Team. $85 million Sales. National Accounts Manager. District Sales Manager. Number One Market Share. Key Account Sales Programs. Joint Venture. Manufacturers Representative Network. Distribution Network.

Client/server architect; systems engineer

Software Engineer. Systems Analyst. Client-Server Architecture. Client-Server Design. Computer Networking. TCP/IP. OSI. GOSIP. Microsoft Exchange. Visual C++/MFC. Visual Basic. OLE Automation. OLE Controls. SQL Server. Sybase.

Oracle. Windows NT. Windows 95. WFW. UNIX. SunOS. Certified Trainer. Certified Systems Engineer. Certified Product Specialist. Designing. Installing. Troubleshooting. SAIC. DISA. AFCEA. BS, Mathematics & Computer Science. Stanford University.

Editor

Technical Editor. Writer. Technical Writer. Editorial Experience. English Major. Copy Editing. Wire Service. IBM. Macintosh. Microsoft Office. Quark XPress. Adobe Photoshop. Adobe Illustrator. Corel Draw. Adobe Pagemaker. Corel WordPerfect. Wire. BA. Literature

Administrative manager

Operations Manager. Director of Administration. Chief Operating Officer. COO. Retail Manager. Public Administration Department Head. General Manager. Management Consultant.

Resources for finding your keywords

- Department of Labor's *Occupational Outlook Handbook* for specific occupations (http://stats.bls.gov/oco/oco1000.htm);
- Employment classifieds of your local newspaper and their online version;
- Job descriptions posted at employer Web sites and specialized job boards;
- Trade journals and magazines for your particular industry or profession;
- *Bluemond's Job Hunter's Word Finder* (see Appendix E).

Examples of skill keywords by job category

The following list of keywords are grouped according to job category. Many of the keywords shown in one job category can certainly overlap into another category. These lists were compiled by the author using a variety of sources mentioned throughout this book and in this appendix.

ACCOUNTANT
— Accounts Payable
— Accounts Receivable
— Audits
— G/L
— Microsoft Excel
— Financial Reports
— SEC Filings
— Budget Analysis
— Gross Margin Analysis
— Month End Closings

ATTORNEY
— Negotiation
— American Bar Association
— Juris Doctor
— Top 10%
— Strategic Planning
— Analytical Abilities
— Counsel
— Legal Writing
— Trial Advocacy
— Research

CIVIL ENGINEER
— American Society of Civil Engineers
— ICBO Certification
— Plans Examiner
— Concrete Design
— Preliminary Stress Analysis
— Hydrology Transportation Analysis
— Land Development Projects
— Scheduling
— AutoCAD
— Public Works

CLERICAL
— Front Desk
— Data Entry
— Reception
— Multiple Phones
— Word Processing
— Database Management
— Filing
— Customer Service
— Time Management
— Document Management

DENTAL HYGIENIST
— General Prophylaxis
— Blood Pressure
— Charting
— Patient Education
— Ultrasonic Scaling
— Nutritional Counseling
— Amalgam Polishing
— Treatment Planning
— Root Planing
— Sealant Application

HUMAN RESOURCES GENERALIST
— EEO Regulations
— ADA
— Applicant Screening
— Applicant Tracking
— 401K
— Merit Pay Program
— Training & Development
— Compensation
— Recruitment
— Diversity

NURSE
— Health Care
— Geriatric
— Preventative Care
— Infection Control
— Teaching
— Bilingual
— EKG
— CPR Certification
— Home Health Care
— Community Outreach

SALES REPRESENTATIVE
— BA/BS
— Exceeded Quota
— Will Travel
— Annual Sales Projections
— Lead Generation
— Customer Support
— Inside Sales
— Account Management

CONSTRUCTION MANAGER
— Building Permit
— Construction Schedule
— Gas Pipeline
— Leveling & Grading
— Job Costs
— Project Specifications
— Subcontractor Management
— Residential Development
— Town & State Permits
— Project Management

ENVIRONMENTAL ENGINEER
— Air Pollution Control
— Emission Compliance
— Groundwater Hydrology
— Municipal Waste
— Environmental Compliance
— Site Assessment
— NEPA
— Superfund
— HAZWOPER
— Asbestos Abatement

MARKETING DIRECTOR
— Strategic Planning Skills
— Market Research
— New Product Transition
— Trade Show Management
— Competitive Market Analysis
— Team Skills
— Multiple Priorities
— Direct Marketing Campaigns
— Business Models
— Marketing Business Plans

OFFICE MANAGER
— Problem-Solving Abilities
— Multi-task Management
— Detail-minded
— Human Relations Skills
— Spreadsheet Development
— Contract Review
— Travel and Meeting Planning
— Vendor Coordination
— Written Communication Skills
— Small Business Environment

SOFTWARE ARCHITECT
— C++
— Knowledge of DDE
— Object-Oriented Design
— Product Design
— 32-bit Environment
— 16-bit Environment
— OLE2 Experience
— Computer Science

CONTRACT ADMINISTRATOR
— Contract Negotiation
— Legal Issues
— Dispute Resolution
— Proposal Preparation
— GSA Schedules
— RFP
— Excellent Oral/Written Communication
— Government Agencies
— Scopes of Work
— Contract Performance

HOTEL MANAGER
— Hospitality Management
— Banquet Sales
— Marketing
— Guest Relations
— Employee Training
— Front Office Management
— Occupancy Rate
— Guest Services
— Convention Management
— Reservations

MEDICAL RECORDS TECHNICIAN
— Medical Terminology
— Patient Statistics
— Transcription
— Dictaphone
— 65 WPM
— Technical Evaluation
— HMO
— Insurance Documentation
— WordPerfect 5.1
— Private Practice

PURCHASING MANAGER
— BS/BA
— Vendor Negotiations
— Reduced Cost
— Improved Quality
— Merchandising
— Wholesale
— Industrial Buyer
— Procurement
— RFQ
— CPM

TEACHER
— Adult Education
— Adult Learning Theory
— GED
— Special Education
— Group Training
— Group Facilitator
— Needs Assessment
— Curriculum Designer

TECHNICAL WRITER
— Copy Editing
— Documentation
— ISO 9000
— Journalism
— User Manuals
— Product Specifications
— Microsoft Office
— FrameMaker 5.0
— PowerPC
— SPARC

TRANSPORTATION MANAGER
— Carrier Negotiation
— Customs Clearance
— Regional Distribution
— Fleet Maintenance
— Operations Management
— Freight Operations
— DOT Regulations
— Inbound Operations
— On-time Delivery
— Outbound Operations

WEB DESIGNER
— Technical Aptitude
— Deadline Driven
— Windows
— Internet Servers
— Page Mill
— HTML
— PDF
— Photoshop
— Creative
— Project Coordination

Personal traits

This list of personal traits was compiled from the same sources used to compile the skill keywords by job category. They were selected based on their frequent occurrence.

— Ability to Delegate
— Analytical
— Conceptual Ability
— Dependable
— Flexible
— High Energy
— Leadership
— Open Minded
— Problem Solving
— Results Oriented
— Self Managing
— Takes Initiative

— Accurate
— Assertive
— Creative
— Detail Minded
— Following Instructions
— Industrious
— Multitasking
— Organizational Skills
— Public Speaking
— Safety Conscious
— Setting Priorities
— Team Player

— Adaptable
— Communication Skills
— Customer Oriented
— Enthusiastic
— Follow Through
— Innovative
— Open Communication
— Presentation Skills
— Resourcefulness
— Self Accountable
— Supportive
— Willing to Travel

Appendix D

Popular Search Engines and Their Indexing Characteristics

The following appendix provides an informational starting point to the use of search engines. It will help you get a feel for what search engines are out there, what kinds of resources are available to you, and online help for implementing Web-page design strategies. Use the search engines to find other people's Web pages and use the critique sheet found on page 99 to guide you. Choose the **View | Source** feature from your Web browser to study HTML tags, such as the <META> and <TITLE> tags used.

Popular search engines

Alta Vista
`http://www.altavista.digital.com`
A keyword index that searches Web pages and newsgroups by keywords.

Onsite Career Hub: Career Zone (`http://www.careeraltavista.com`) lets you search for resumes and jobs, and post resumes and jobs directly from the Alta Vista Web site.

Excite
`http://www.excite.com`
A hybrid keyword index and subject directory, searches Web pages by keywords, categories, and concepts.

Onsite Career Hub: Excite provides guides under the category "careers/education" at `http://my.excite.com/careers_and_education`. Use Excite to access The Monster Board to find a job and build a resume. You can also use it to set up a personal job-search agent. Or, if you are hiring, you can post a job on the Online Career Center.

HotBot
`http://www.hotbot.com`
A keyword index that searches Web pages by keywords.

Onsite Career Hub: The CareerBuilder Network (`http://www.careerbuilder.com`).

Infoseek

http://www.infoseek.com

Infoseek combines both indexing and directories. It is a full-text keyword index that searches Web pages using natural language queries.

Onsite Career Hub: Careerpath.com (http://www.careerpath.com) helps you find jobs, post resumes, and post jobs.

Lycos

http://www.lycos.com

A keyword index suited for simple searches by keywords on common topics.

Onsite Career Hub: Careers Web Guide (http://www.lycos.com/careers) and CareerMosaic (http://www.careermosaic.lycos.com) can help search for jobs and post resumes.

Magellan

http://www.mckinley.com

Searches by keywords and by concept. Magellan looks for documents containing the words you enter into the query box, and also looks for ideas related to the words in your query.

Onsite Career Hub: Site reviews are listed under the Business Jobs category (http://www.mckinley.com/magellan/Reviews/Business/Jobs/index.magellan.html).

Northern Light

http://www.nlsearch.com

A keyword index search engine that organizes information by topic. Also provides an expanded "special collections" category of more refined Web documents that can be accessed for a fee.

Onsite Career Hub: Search for topics by industry and jobs by industry from the Industry tab of the homepage (http://www.northernlight.com/industry.html).

Yahoo!

http://www.yahoo.com

A subject directory that searches by subject on common information, including Usenet newsgroups and e-mail addresses that you want to find quickly. Ideal for searching for Web pages by categories.

Onsite Career Hub: Yahoo! Classifieds Employment by metro or state: (http://classifieds.yahoo.com/employment.html). This is not a direct link to employment wanted; you need to register in the Submit Ad area first (http://edit.classifieds.yahoo.com/51/submit?cc=forhire).

Metasearch Engines

Search multiple search engines at once with these metasearch engines:

Dogpile

http://www.dogpile.com

MetaCrawler
http://www.metacrawler.com

Savvy Search
http://www.savvysearch.com

General search engine guides

Danny Sullivan's SearchEngine Watch
http://www.searchenginewatch.com

Provides an excellent Webmaster's guide to search engines. It explains how search engines find and rank Web pages, and what you can do to improve how search engines list your Web site.

Findspot
http://www.findspot.com

Findspot is a gateway to free Internet search tools that help users construct better searches and locate information easily on the Internet.

Virtual Stampede's Expert's Choice Web Site Secrets and Search Engine Update Newsletter
http://virtual-stampede.com

This site offers tips for online traffic-building, marketing, and promotion strategies.

Search engines and <META> tags

Use the following resources to fine-tune your <META> tags:

HotWired's Webmonkey
http://www.hotwired.com/webmonkey/html/96/51/index2a.html

Melissa Wisner's Search Engines and Their Descriptions
http://cortex.uchc.edu/~mwisner/engines.html

Virtual Stampede's Web Site Traffic Building Strategies that Work
http://virtual-stampede.com

Home of Expert's Choice Web Site Secrets and Search Engine Update Newsletter.

WebCrawler's discussion on WWW Robots, Wanderers, and Spiders
http://info.Webcrawler.com/mak/projects/robots/robots.html

Web page announcement resources

"Hits" on your Web page are the number of people who access your Web page...and the more hits the better! Use announcement services to get more people looking at your resume.

AddURL
http://www.addurl.com

Submit your URL to 500 search engines all at once.

Submit-it
http://www.submit-it.com

Used by 250,000-plus Web masters from Fortune 500 employees to hobbyists.

Submit URL
http://www.webthemes.com/submit.html

This site promotes your home page by sending your URL to 2,000 places!

WebStep Top 100
http://www.mmgco.com/top100.html

Web Step links to the best 100 places that will list your Web site for free.

Appendix E

Suggested Reading

Book reading

The books listed here can be found online as well, through Amazon.com (http://www.amazon.com) and Barnes and Noble (http://www.barnesandnoble.com), or from the publisher's Web sites directly. Refer to these sites for the latest editions.

Shifting Gears: Thriving in the New Economy; Nuala Beck, HarperCollins, 1996; ISBN 0006384803

Downsizing. Unemployment. However gloomy the outlook, the world is not coming to an end economically—it's just changing. This optimistic book discusses how job-seekers can benefit from this transition. The "new economy" emerging will be built by "knowledge workers," those with the skills and knowledge necessary to adjust to constant change.

Resumes! Resumes! Resumes!; The editors of Career Press, 1997; ISBN 1564143090

The third edition of *Resumes! Resumes! Resumes!* covers all the basics of resume writing and gives dozens of samples from the country's top pros. Heads of the biggest personnel agencies, recruiting firms as well as career authors and columnists, share their favorite resumes—ones that will land you a job—and explain why they work.

Cover Letters! Cover Letters! Cover Letters!; Richard Fein, Career Press, 1997; ISBN 1564142620

This book is for anyone on the job-search trail, from new college grads to veteran managers. This new edition includes more detailed advice and the most up-to-date samples of every kind of job-related letter—from letters following up on interviews to those rejecting a job offer.

Electronic Resume Revolution: Creating a Winning Resume for the New World of Job Seeking; Joyce Lain Kennedy and Thomas J. Morrow, John Wiley & Sons, 1995; ISBN 0471115762

Kennedy and Morrow's book explains in detail how different scanning systems, such as Resumix, Restrac, and SmartSearch2 work. It also suggests the optimum kinds of resumes for each kind of system that will maximize your chances of getting "picked up" by them.

Power Resumes; Ron Tepper, John Wiley & Sons, 1998; ISBN 0471247812

This was *the* book that made the difference in writing my own resume, as well as helping to write resumes for others. Tepper's power resume approach consists of identifying value-added benefits that show a hiring manager what you as the applicant can add to the bottom line. It shows you how to carefully match your qualifications with the requirements of top jobs using 10 power resume ingredients that can also be incorporated into your job search.

Electronic Resumes for the New Job Market; Peter D. Weddle, Impact Publications, 1994; ISBN 1570230080

This book is based on the practical experience of Peter Weddle, president of Job Bank USA, an electronic resume database company. Weddle does an excellent job of describing the importance of an electronic resume within the context of a new job market that consists of warp speed jobs, high definition skills, and free agent employees.

Cybercareers: A 21st Century Guide to Emerging Careers; Mary E.S. Morris and Paul Massie, Sun Microsystems Press, 1998; ISBN 0137488726

If you are planning a career in the 21st century, you'll need skills in cyberspace literacy, communications, and the ability to manage change and think "out-of-the-box." This practical book describes how the Internet will dramatically change the world of work, and what you need to do to stay employed in it.

Portfolio Power: The New Way to Showcase All Your Job Skills and Experiences; Martin Kimeldorf, Peterson's, 1997; ISBN 1560797614

This is probably the only book of its kind that pinpoints an often over-looked job search tool: portfolios. The Web is the perfect medium to incorporate items once considered taboo in traditional paper resumes. The portfolio takes the graphic impact of your e-resume and augments it by showing your skills in progress.

Be Your Own Online Headhunter; Get the Job You Want Using the Information Superhighway; Pam Dixon and Sylvia Tiersten, Random House, 1995; ISBN 0679761934

This is the first guide devoted to showing how to use the resources of the Internet to conduct a national or international job-search; keep current in your field; find top experts; track the competition; use online resources to prepare for job interviews; and connect with major employers through electronic job banks.

More books and magazines

Here is a collection of easy to understand books and periodicals found in bookstores and on the Web:

Alta Vista Search Revolution: How to Find Anything on the Internet; Richard Seltzer, Eric J. Ray, et al., Osborne/McGraw-Hill, 1998; ISBN 0078822351

The Complete Idiot's Guide to Creating an HTML 4 Web Page; Paul McFedries, Que, 1997; ISBN 0789714906

Creating Great Web Graphics; Laurie McCanna, IDG Books Worldwide, 1997; ISBN 1558285504

Designing for the Web: Getting Started in a New Medium; Jennifer Niederst, O'Reilly, ISBN 1565921658

Getting Hits: The Definitive Guide to Promoting Your Website; Don Sellers, Peachpit Press, 1997, ISBN 0201688158

HTML for Dummies; Ed Tittel and Steve James, IDG Books Worldwide, 1997; ISBN 076450214X

Increase Your Web Traffic in a Weekend; William R. Stanek; Prima Publishing, 1997; ISBN 0761511946

Internet File Formats; Tim Kientzle, Coriolis Group Books, 1995; ISBN 188357756X

Official Microsoft FrontPage 98 Book; Kerry A Lehto and W. Brett Polonsky, Microsoft Press, 1997; ISBN 1572316292

Web Site Stats; Rick Stout, Osborne/McGraw-Hill, 1997; ISBN 007882236X

The World Wide Web for Busy People; Stephen L. Nelson, Osborne/McGraw-Hill, 1996; ISBN 0078812440

Web reading

Newsgroups

Go to `http://www.neosoft.com/internet/paml/index.html` to find a searchable index of mailing lists (go to the bottom of the page and click on **Search**). This page also has a link to other mailing list resources that you should check out.

The long, complicated process of creating an official newsgroup is explained at `http://www.fairnet.org/fnvol/training/newsgrp.html` and a good reference about unofficial newsgroups is at `http://www.cis.ohio-state.edu/~barr/alt-creation-guide.html`

The Riley Guide's Using Newsgroups and Mailing Lists
`http://www.dbm.com/jobguide/post.html`

Electronic file formats

There are several Web pages that people have created to help provide information about the various file formats. These are useful reference points, because they can keep you abreast of the latest viewing and conversion utilities as well.

The Ultimate Macintosh
http://www.freepress.com/myee/umac.html

This is a good guide to Macintosh resources on the World Wide Web.

Common Internet File Formats
http://www.matisse.net/files/formats.html

A comprehensive listing of file formats with their description and type, with corresponding hyperlinks to manipulate the respective file formats. There is also a link to an FAQ on file compression.

The Graphics File Formats Page
http://www.dcs.ed.ac.uk/~mxr/gfx

Of special interest here is the link to FAQs on managing Internet graphics file formats conversion and compression.

Electronic mail

To find out more about how e-mail programs handle attachments, try visiting some of these online resources and tutorials:

Vanderbilt University's Attachment Resolver
http://www.vanderbilt.edu/vumail/resolver.html

A convenient tool to get you started. Simply select the categories for either receiving or sending an attachment, select the software being used, and then select the **How do I do this?** button.

Earthlink's How to use Microsoft Outlook for Internet Mail
http://www.earthlink.net/daily/thursday/outlook

Step-by-step instructions on how to set up Microsoft Outlook.

The RMIT University, Melbourne, Australia Eudora Light Tutorial
http://www.srl.rmit.edu.au/pd/wineudl/index.html

Eudora Light is a popular shareware program used for sending and receiving e-mail. This tutorial has been online quite awhile, taking you through the main features of Eudora that make handling e-mail easier, including how to manage attachments.

VSchool.Net Userguide
http://www.vschool.net/userguide/software

Provides several links to setting up and using some of the popular e-mail programs such as Pegasus, Eudora, and Netscape Communicator for both the PC and the Macintosh.

The Authoritative Encyclopedia of Computing
http://www.mcp.com

Presented by Macmillan Publishing, access the Internet Starter Kit by Adam C. Engst. This entire book is online for both Microsoft Windows and the Macintosh.

You can find comprehensive detail on using e-mail. Access the book from the "Resource Centers" link from the home page, select "General Internet," and then select the "Internet Starter Kit" link.

Anti-virus information

To fight off infection, try using one of these popular virus scanners:

Touchstone's PC-cillin Anti-Virus
http://www.checkit.com

A popular anti-virus software product. This site also provides a unique technical support chat room where you can learn more about those annoying viruses.

Macvirus
http://www.macvirus.com

A Macintosh anti-virus resource. A comprehensive site containing Macintosh virus software updates, as well as news and articles.

McAfee's VirusScan
http://www.mcafee.com

Another popular anti-virus software product, this site provides and extensive online library of virus information.

ZDNet
http://www.zdnet.com

Search ZDNet with keyword "virus." Provides excellent coverage on the nature of viruses, and product reviews of all the latest antiviral software.

Rob Rosenberger's Computer Virus Myths
http://kumite.com/myths

An interesting look at the myths behind viruses hiding inside a data file, in e-mail, or in the text of a worldwide Web page.

Web Page Design Resources

These guides provide additional resources for the novice Web designer:

How to Avoid 10 Fatal Website Mistakes
http://www.techweb.com/netbiz/archives/inter0204steps.html

Internet Baglady
http://www.dumpsterdive.com

Tutorials, templates, and tips to help you create content on a budget.

PC Magazine's The Best 100 Web Sites
http://www.zdnet.com/pcmag/special/web100/index.html

Sun Microsystem's Guide to Web Style
http://www.sun.com/styleguide

The 1998 Webby Awards
http://www.webbyawards.com

Top Ten Ways to Tell If You Have A Sucky Home Page
http://www.glover.com/sucky.html
Vincent & Michael's "Web Pages that Suck."

Web Design Tips for New Web Developers
http://www.ochin.on.ca/webdesign

Web page graphics resources

Search the Yahoo! directory (http://www.yahoo.com) to find more links to images in the public domain:

Animated GIFs
http://www.yahoo.com/Arts/Visual_Arts/Animation/Computer_Animation/Animated_GIFs

Background Images
http://www.yahoo.com/Computers_and_Internet/Internet/World_Wide_Web/Page_Design_and_Layout/Graphics/Backgrounds

Clip Art
http://www.yahoo.com/Computers_and_Internet/Graphics/Clip_Art

Here are a few more Web resources for free images and image information:

Clip Art Searcher
http://www.webplaces.com/search
Search for more than 650,000 images on the Web.

Internet World's Graphic Toolbox: Five Tricks for Terrific Backgrounds
http://www.internetworld.com/daily/tips/1998/02/0301-tricks.html

The Mining Company's Web Clipart index
http://webclipart.miningco.com

HTML tutorials and Web page builders

Here's everything you wanted to know about HTML, and then some:

Angelfire Free Homepage Editor
http://www.angelfire.com

Free Homepage Center
http://www.freehomepage.com/main.htm

Geocities (free home pages and e-mail)
http://www.geocities.com

HTML for Beginners
http://www.cnet.com/Content/Builder/Authoring/Basics

HTML Tips & Tricks
http://www.cnet.com/Content/Builder/Authoring/Htmltips

Kevin Werbach's The Bare Bones Guide
http://werbach.com/barebones/barebone.txt

Microsoft's SiteBuilder Network
http://www.microsoft.com/workshop/contents.asp

Microsoft's SiteBuilder Network: Dynamic HTML Gallery for Internet Explorer 4.0
http://www.microsoft.com/gallery/files/html

Official HTML Specifications
http://www.w3.org/MarkUp/MarkUp.html

Tripod's Free Homepage Builder
http://homepager.tripod.com

Writing HTML: A Tutorial for Creating WWW Pages
http://www.mcli.dist.maricopa.edu/tut/lessons.html

XOOM Free Easy Page Builder
http://www.xoom.com

Appendix F

HTML Tags and Attributes

HTML Tags and Attributes	Examples

HTML Document Structure
 	
`<HEAD>` always precedes `<TITLE>` and other comment tags, followed by the closing `</HEAD>`tag.
	`<HTML>`
	`<HEAD>`
	`<TITLE>    Welcome    to    California    </TITLE>`
	`</HEAD>`
	`<BODY>`
	`... [ Body of Web page ]`
	`</BODY>`
	`</HTML>`

HTML Structure Tags Opening and closing tags indicate where a piece of text begins and ends.	`<HTML></HTML>, <HEAD></HEAD>, <BODY></BODY>`

Heading and Title Tags	`<H1></H1>,   <H2></H2>,   <H3></H3>,   <H4></H4>,`
	`<H5></H5>, <H6></H6>`
	
	`<TITLE></TITLE>    Always    used    within    the`
	`<HEAD></HEAD>` tag pair of an HTML document.

Paragraph Tags	`<P></P>` Creates a new paragraph by inserting a blank line between paragraphs. Closing tag is optional, but recommended.
List Tags	`<UL></UL>` Bulleted list. `<OL></OL>` Numbered list. `<LI>` List item
Link Tags	`<A></A>` (see also HTML Attributes)
Miscellaneous Tags	` ` forces a line break but does not insert a blank line. `<CENTER></CENTER>` Center align the enclosed text. `<HR>` Horizontal rule. `<BLINK></BLINK>` Blinking text. `<FONT></FONT>` Changes the format of the font used for the enclosed text. Attributes include SIZE, FACE, and COLOR.
Comment Tags Comments placed between these tags do not appear on the actual Web page when viewed in a Web browser. They only appear when the source HTML code is viewed. It is recommended that you not include HTML coding (that is, other tags) within start and endbrackets.	`<META>` Provides information about the page itself — including SUBJECT, AUTHOR, CONTENT, and KEYWORDS — that search engines and software agents use to index and retrieve documents. `<COMMENT><!type    comments    here></COMMENT>` Provides plain explanations so that anyone reviewing the source HTML code can interpret it. `<!DOCTYPE>` Recommended by the World Wide Web Consortium (W3C) to place at the beginning of all Web pages so that software, such as browsers, can identify whether the document conforms to current HTML standards.

HTML Tags and Attributes	Examples
Character Formatting Tags	`<I></I>` Italic text.
	`<B></B>` Bold text.
Graphics Tags	`<IMG SRC=>`
	`<BODY BACKGROUND="IMAGE.JPG">`
HTML Attributes Attributes are special code words usually enclosed in quote marks used inside the brackets to control tags.	`ALIGN="..."` Used with the `<P></P>` tag pair. Possible variables are `LEFT`, `RIGHT`, and `CENTER`. `HREF="..."`, `NAME="..."` Used with the `<A></A>` tag pair. `HREF` creates a link to another document or anchor; `NAME` creates an anchor to which a link may be made. `SRC="..."` Used with the `<IMG>` tag, which specifies the source URL of an image.

Glossary

ASCII

American Standard Code for Information Interchange. The text language that computer software programs use to communicate with each other.

Bookmarks

In a Web browser, a list of your favorite Web pages.

Browser

The software you use to display and interact with a Web page. Microsoft Internet Explorer and Netscape Navigator are the two most popular browsers.

Carriage Return

In an ASCII file, a carriage return indicates a line break. In a word processor file, a carriage return usually indicates the end of a paragraph. Carriage returns are also referred to as hard returns.

Chat

A way of having quick, immediate, back-and-forth conversations on the Internet. Chatting is much like talking on the telephone, with the fundamental difference being that you are typing instead of talking.

Default

Used in reference to the choice made by a program when the user does not specify an alternative. Defaults are built into programs if some value or option needs to be assumed in order for the program to function.

E-mail

Electronic Mail. The transmission of messages over a communications network. Messages can be sent to anywhere in the world to a specific e-mail address.

FAQ

Frequently Asked Questions. It is a list of questions that, over the history of a discussion forum or a Web site, have come up most often.

FTP

File Transfer Protocol. An electronic standard used to transfer files from one location on the Internet to another.

GIF

Graphics Interchange Format. The most commonly used graphics format on the Web.

Gopher

A menu system that helps to locate and use resources on the Internet. A Gopher menu is typically used to search for and transfer binary files.

Hard Copy

The original printed paper copy of the resume.

HTML

HyperText Markup Language. Codes embedded in an ASCII file to format text, insert graphics, add borders, etc. HTML sets up the way a Web page appears on a browser.

Hypertext

A metaphor for the presenting of information in which text, images, sounds, and actions become linked together in a complex, nonsequential web of associations. These computer-linked associations permit the user to browse through related topics, regardless of the presented order. *See also* **Link**.

Internet

Originally referred to as "internetworking," the Internet is a network of thousands of computers sending and receiving information all over the world. The Internet is affectionately nicknamed the "Net" or the "Information Superhighway."

Jargon

Specialized terms or phrases unique to those who are in a particular field or profession. Past advice regarding the use of jargon in the body of resumes was discouraged. Electronic resumes now require it.

JPEG

Joint Photographic Experts Group. A common Web graphics format developed by the Joint Photographic Experts Group.

Link

A word, phrase or image that, when selected, sends the reader to a different location on the same Web page, or to another page altogether on the Web.

Mailing List

A "newsletter" of sorts where people can discuss a topic and send their response to a list of "subscribers."

Message Board

A designated place online where people can post messages for others to see. In the case of the term "job boards," these are Web pages where employers can post job announcements for potential candidates to view, much like the way you would thumbtack a job announcement on a traditional bulletin board. Many online discussion forums provide areas where you can post messages regarding to a specific topic.

Netiquette

An informal set of rules and guidelines designed to streamline interaction among participants in a discussion forum or users of a Web site. *See also* **FAQ**.

Newsgroup

Newgroups are like giant bulletin boards. People tack up (or "post") messages, and anyone with simple software, such as a newsreader found on most Web browsers, and Internet access can read them. People can reply as well, and most newsgroup software can easily sort the messages by topic. These topics are called "threads."

Online

The place you "go to" when you connect to the Internet to reach out beyond your own computer (usually via modem) and interact with information or people on other computer systems.

RTF

Rich Text Format. Standard format first introduced by Microsoft used to retain formatted code information while transferring word processing files between different word processors.

Soft Copy

Refers to the electronic form of the resume that is displayed on a computer screen.

URL

Uniform Resource Locator. A unique address that points to Web sites on the Internet, files, newsgroups, Gopher sites, and FTP sites. A URL is a one-line address on the Internet (`http://www.eresumes.com`, for example).

World Wide Web

Also referred to as the Web, or the WWW, it is that portion of the Internet that is a system of documents containing text, graphics, and other multimedia.

About the Author

Rebecca Smith is an established Web author, adult education teacher, and columnist who has been monitoring technology and its impact on the job market for the past 10 years. Her Web site, www.eresumes.com was selected as one of Lycos's Top 5 Percent Career Guides for Winners. She has held positions in technology and personnel management for business and government.

Index